As puppet presentations continue to grow in popularity, churches, children's groups and special ministries have joined in to use this enchanting visual medium.

MORE PUPPET DIALOGUES is the sequel to the popular PUPPET DIALOGUES, presenting 24 more Bible stories through tested skits which will delight and teach young and old alike.

MORE PUPPET DIALOGUES

Charles E. Magnet

ACCENT BOOKS
Denver, Colorado

MEMBER OF
EVANGELICAL CHRISTIAN
PUBLISHERS ASSOCIATION

ACCENT BOOKS
A division of Accent-B/P Publications, Inc.
12100 W. Sixth Avenue
P.O. Box 15337
Denver, Colorado 80215

Library of Congress Catalog Number: 79-53446

ISBN 0-89636-035-0

CONTENTS

FOREWORD

More Puppet Dialogues is a continuation of my previous book, *Puppet Dialogues*. In this new volume I have tried to be as true to Biblical content as before. I do not believe that puppet dialogue for church use, if it is to teach the Bible, can be any less than Biblical in its content. The great need for this hour is more and better Bible teaching in our churches. It is my desire that these puppet dialogues will help do just that.

In this book you will recognize some of your old friends such as Tammy, Annabelle, Betty and Freddie. In addition to these I have added some new characters. There is Gertrude, Wayne, Susie and Uncle Charlie. Our old friend Grumpy Herman has such a change of heart that he becomes Happy Herman.

The length of the dialogues remains about the same. Most of the dialogues require two or three puppet characters with a few going to four. I have kept in mind that for the beginning puppet program there is a need for fewer puppet characters, and yet I believe that these dialogues could be suited to the most advanced puppet ministry.

Most of the dialogues in this book have been used in a children's worship setting or children's rally, and it has proved to be a great success with the children that I have worked with. To a limited degree some of this material has been used even in an adult setting such as church-wide fellowships and sweetheart banquets. I have come to discover that a puppet ministry is a ministry to all ages if it teaches the Bible.

It is my prayer that the puppeteers who use this material might find it useful in their own lives as well as for the audiences for which they perform. It is also my prayer that this book will be just one of the many aids and tools that will help in strengthening the great work of the local church.

Charles E. Magnet
Pastor's Study
West Hendersonville Baptist Church
Hendersonville, N.C.

To my dear wife, Carolyn
and my children
Janice, David, and Charles, Jr.

ACKNOWLEDGMENTS

I would like to express my appreciation to all of those who have had a part in making these volumes possible. First of all to my dear wife, Carolyn, who has been so faithful in taking dictation for these dialogues. To my children, Charles, David and Janice for their cooperation during the writing of these dialogues. To those who typed the dialogues at one time or the other, Janice Hyder, Wayne Johnson, Margie Massey, and to Betty Sitton who typed the final manuscript. To the children who listened weekly to these programs in our very own children's worship service. To Carolyn Vaughan, our children's worship director. To our faithful puppeteers, Gregg Newman, Kim Sitton, Alex Redden, Shirley McNeil. Last but not least, to the West Hendersonville Fellowship, who have allowed me the time and setting in which to do this work.

GOD'S WONDERFUL CREATION

Scripture:	**Genesis 1**
Characters:	**2 Puppets, 1 girl and 1 boy**

HONEY: [*Both puppets come onstage together.*] Oh dear me, Sonny, I just think everything is so beautiful this time of the year, don't you?

SONNY: Why yes, Honey, I do. Spring is always a beautiful time of the year.

HONEY: Oh yes, oh yes, oh yes. It really is. All of the flowers are beginning to bloom and the trees are getting green.

SONNY: Oh yes, and it's getting warm too. And oh yes, it won't be long until school will be out.

HONEY: And what's wrong with school?

SONNY: Well after eight months it gets tiresome.

HONEY: Oh Sonny, I think it's fun to go to school. But I do like when vacation time comes. Summer time is always a fun time.

SONNY: It sure is, Honey. But you know any time of the year can be a fun time in God's creation — the world. And you know He created it for us.

HONEY: Yes Sonny, He really did and the Bible explains it all.

SONNY: Yes, the Bible really does. Honey, do you suppose the boys and girls would like to hear the story of God's creation of the world and the plants and the animals?

HONEY: Oh yes, oh yes, oh yes. I do believe they would and I know I would. Wouldn't you, boys and girls?

SONNY: All right, here we go. The Bible says in Genesis the first chapter the very first verse that in the beginning God created all things.

HONEY: That really means everything too, doesn't it Sonny? And He created it all in six days, didn't He?

SONNY: Yes to both of your questions. God created everything in six days.

HONEY:	Sonny, do you believe God created it in six days like we have today?
SONNY:	Yes I do, Honey. I believe that He created all of this world, its animals and even man in six days just like we know it today.
HONEY:	Wow! Wow! Wow! God sure is great!
SONNY:	He sure is. Now if you'll quit interrupting me I'll get on with the story.
HONEY:	Oh, I'm sorry. Please do go on.
SONNY:	Well, in the beginning the earth was one big mess. It was all dark; there was a lot of water and God said let their be light and there was light.
HONEY:	You mean it was dark all of the time?
SONNY:	Yes, and God divided the light from the darkness and He called the light day and the darkness He called night.
HONEY:	So on the first day God created day and night, didn't He?
SONNY:	That's right, Honey, He sure did.
HONEY:	What happened on the second day?
SONNY:	Well, on the second day God divided the waters, and He made the oceans below and the sky above.
HONEY:	Oh dear, oh dear. It is just hard to imagine the beautiful blue sky never being here. And all the pretty white clouds that look like cotton candy.
SONNY:	Yes, they almost look good enough to eat sometimes.
HONEY:	Yes, and they're so funny looking sometimes. They look like people. Well, what happened next?
SONNY:	Well, on the third day, God made the oceans to stay in one place, and out of what was left He made land. Then God created the grass and plants and fruit trees and he even put seeds inside of the fruit so they would produce the kinds of fruit and plants they came from.
HONEY:	Oh my, how wonderful. God thought of everything. And all of this happened on the third day, didn't it?
SONNY:	That's right, Honey. Now on the fourth day God hung up the

sun and He hung up the moon and He also threw out the stars.

HONEY: How many stars are there, Sonny? Are there more than a hundred?

SONNY: Oh dear me, oh my. Oh dear me, oh my. There's no way to count the stars. It would be like trying to count the sand down at the beach. And that's impossible.

HONEY: Wow! Wow! You can sure say that again. Well, what happened on the fifth day?

SONNY: Man, things really began to happen on the fifth day. God said let the water be filled with fish and then there were lots of fish.

HONEY: You mean like catfish and dogfish and flying fish?

SONNY: Yes, I mean all those kinds of fish. I mean every kind of fish.

HONEY: Do you even mean walking fish?

SONNY: Yes indeed, Honey, I even mean walking fish. Did you know that there is even a walking catfish that God created?

HONEY: Oh yes, and I sure wouldn't want to meet one on a dark night. What else did God create on the fifth day?

SONNY: Well, He created the birds that fly away up high in the sky. And that was the end of the fifth day.

HONEY: Oh dear, God is so wonderful. Please hurry on and tell us what happened on the sixth day.

SONNY: Well, on the sixth day, God created all the animals and the cattle and even the reptiles.

HONEY: What in the world is a reptile?

SONNY: Honey, you mean you don't know what a reptile is?

HONEY: Well is it a rip in the tile like on the floor?

SONNY: Boy, Honey, you're not too smart.

HONEY: Well, Mr. Smarty, what is a reptile?

SONNY: Why it's a snake. That's what a reptile is.

HONEY: Oh dear, oh dear, snakes. Uh, I think I'm going to faint.

SONNY: Well, why in the world do you think you're going to faint?

HONEY: Because I'm scared of snakes that's why.

SONNY: There aren't any snakes around here, don't be silly.

HONEY: Are you sure? [*She looks around suspiciously.*]

SONNY: Why, sure I'm sure. Now let me get on with the story.

HONEY: Yes, please do.

SONNY: Next, God made man and then He made a woman.

HONEY: Their names were Adam and Eve and they were the first husband and wife in all the world.

SONNY: That's right, Honey. Adam and Eve were the first man and woman. And they were the first husband and wife and the first mother and father in all the world. Then it was the end of the sixth day.

HONEY: God rested on the seventh day, didn't He?

SONNY: Why, yes He did, Honey. And God wants us to have a day of rest and for Christians it is Sunday.

HONEY: God thought of everything, didn't He?

SONNY: He sure did, Honey.

HONEY: That was a real good story. I know the boys and girls really liked it. I really did.

SONNY: Well, thank you, Honey. I really like to tell Bible stories because the Bible is God's Word and all the stories in the Bible are true stories.

HONEY: Let's go Sonny and enjoy all of God's creations.

SONNY: That would sure be neat, Honey. Boys and girls, we will see you again real soon.

TOGETHER: Bye now. [*Both Puppets exit together.*]

THE FIRST SIN

Scripture:	Genesis 3:1-24
Characters:	2 Puppets, 1 boy and 1 girl

BETTY: [*Betty comes onstage talking to herself.*] Oh dear me, oh my. So many problems. People being mean. Oh dear me. How terrible, how terrible.

FREDDIE: [*Freddie comes onstage.*] Betty, what in the world is so terrible?

BETTY: Oh, Freddie. I didn't see you come in. What is so terrible? You mean you don't know?

FREDDIE: No, Betty, I don't know what is so terrible. I think everything's fine.

BETTY: Oh, Freddie, you never see anything wrong.

FREDDIE: Well, are you going to tell me what's wrong or not?

BETTY: Oh, Freddie. It's just the world. People fighting and all kinds of those terrible things. Don't you think it's terrible?

FREDDIE: Oh yes. I think all of that is terrible.

BETTY: Well, why does it have to be that way? Why can't everyone love everyone else?

FREDDIE: Dear me, Betty. If everyone was a Christian we wouldn't have these problems. It's sin that causes the problems in our world.

BETTY: Oh, I wish there had never been any sin.

FREDDIE: Well I do too, Betty. But sin is the cause of all of our troubles and problems. Sin is the reason the Lord Jesus had to come and die on the cross.

BETTY: Oh, I just wish what's-her-name had not eaten that apple.

FREDDIE: You mean Eve?

BETTY: Yes, that's who it was. It was Eve. I wish Eve had not eaten that apple.

FREDDIE: Betty, who in the world told you that Eve ate an apple.

15

BETTY:	Well, I don't really know. But she did, didn't she?
FREDDIE:	Well now, Betty, the Bible doesn't say so.
BETTY:	Well, what did happen?
FREDDIE:	Betty, how would you like to hear the story of the first sin? I think it would help you understand just what happened.
BETTY:	Yes, I'm certain it would. Would you please tell me?
FREDDIE:	Our story begins in the beautiful garden of Eden. The first man and the first woman lived there in that beautiful garden.
BETTY:	Did they live all by themselves?
FREDDIE:	Oh dear me no, Betty, there were all kinds of animals that lived in the garden with them.
BETTY:	Were Adam and Eve not afraid?
FREDDIE:	Oh dear me no. You see, there was no sin in the world then. And the animals were not wild or mean.
BETTY:	Oh how wonderful that must have been. Let's get on with the story.
FREDDIE:	Betty, if you will just get quiet, I will.
BETTY:	Sorry.
FREDDIE:	One day while Eve was alone in a part of the garden, a serpent began to talk to her.
BETTY:	What's a serpent?
FREDDIE:	It's a snake.
BETTY:	I didn't know snakes could talk.
FREDDIE:	They can't.
BETTY:	But I thought you said the snake talked to Eve.
FREDDIE:	I did. But it was the devil that was speaking through the snake.
BETTY:	Oh, now I see. What did the snake say to Eve?

FREDDIE:	He asked if she could not eat of all the fruit in the garden. Eve said she could, but one, God would not allow . . .
BETTY:	Ah, ha. I know what tree that was. It was the apple tree.
FREDDIE:	Now wait just a minute, Betty. The Bible doesn't say that it was an apple tree.
BETTY:	Well, what was it then?
FREDDIE:	Well, the Bible says that it was the tree of knowledge of good and evil. But the kind of fruit it had on it, the Bible just doesn't tell us.
BETTY:	Well, why weren't they supposed to eat it?
FREDDIE:	Well, Eve told the snake that God said they should not eat it because if they did they would die.
BETTY:	Oh dear me. What did the snake have to say about all of that?
FREDDIE:	"That is a big fat lie," the snake hissed to Eve. "You'll not die but you'll become like God."
BETTY:	Oh dear me. That snake really talked ugly, didn't he?
FREDDIE:	Betty, everything about the devil is ugly. If people could just see it.
BETTY:	What did Eve do next?
FREDDIE:	Eve began to look at the tree and she decided if it would make her wise like God she would just go ahead and eat some of it.
BETTY:	Oh dear me. She did eat it, didn't she?
FREDDIE:	Yes, she did, Betty. And then she gave some to her husband, Adam, to eat. And he ate it.
BETTY:	Oh dear me. What happened to them? Did they die?
FREDDIE:	Well, the first thing that happened, they looked at each other and for the first time since God had created them, they were ashamed because they were both naked.
BETTY:	You mean they didn't know it before?
FREDDIE:	No, because they didn't have any sin in their life.
BETTY:	Well, then did they die?

FREDDIE:	No, they didn't die right then. They just got old and died but if they had not sinned they would have lived forever and ever in the beautiful garden.
BETTY:	Oh dear. How terrible sin is.
FREDDIE:	Yes, it is, Betty. Adam and Eve had to leave the beautiful garden because of their sin.
BETTY:	Oh, that was just terrible.
FREDDIE:	Now, Betty, do you understand how sin came into the world?
BETTY:	I sure do, Freddie. Now I understand why people fight and why they hate each other.
FREDDIE:	But, Betty, don't ever forget that God sent his Son, Jesus, into the world so people could love each other.
BETTY:	Yes, that's true, Freddie. My favorite verse is John 3:16.
FREDDIE:	Betty, would you share that verse with everyone? It's my favorite, too.
BETTY:	I would be delighted to. "For God so loved the world, that he gave his only begotten Son, that whosoever believeth in him should not perish, but have everlasting life."
FREDDIE:	Betty, that really makes us feel better to know God loves us, doesn't it?
BETTY:	It sure does, Freddie, and you know I feel much better after that wonderful Bible story and after thinking about John 3:16.
FREDDIE:	Betty, I guess I'd better be going.
BETTY:	Wait for me. I'll go with you. I sure wouldn't want to meet a serpent by myself. [Both Puppets exit.]

DEPARTING FOR HEAVEN

Scripture: Genesis 5:21-24; II Kings 2:1-11
Characters: 2 Puppets, 2 girls

BETTY: *[Both puppets come onstage together.]* Hello there boys and girls. It's just so good to see you today and I want to introduce you to my little niece Annabelle. Say hello to the boys and girls, Annabelle.

ANNABELLE: Hello, boys and girls. It's so good to see you. Hee, hee, hee, hee.

BETTY: Annabelle, how do you like our Children's Worship and all of these fine looking boys and girls?

ANNABELLE: Well, Aunt Betty, I like Children's Worship just fine. I don't know about the girls but the boys sure are fine looking. Hee, hee, hee, hee.

BETTY: Why, Annabelle, shame on you. All of these boys and girls are fine looking.

ANNABELLE: Oh, I guess you're right, Aunt Betty. Aunt Betty, there's something that's been bothering me.

BETTY: Well, what in the world is it, child?

ANNABELLE: Well, the other day I overheard some big people in our church talking about two men who went to heaven without dying. Is that really so, Aunt Betty?

BETTY: Well, indeed it is child. Yes, indeedy, deed, deed it is.

ANNABELLE: Well, who was it?

BETTY: Well, Annabelle, one of them was a man by the name of Enoch and the other one was the prophet Elijah.

ANNABELLE: Well, I've never heard of Mr. Knock or Sock or whoever you said but I sure do know about Mr. Elijah.

BETTY: Oh dear me, child. His name was Enoch and what do you know about Elijah?

ANNABELLE: Well, I think that some horses on fire came down to get him or something like that.

BETTY:	Oh dear me, child. Dear me. You're all confused. I think that I need to tell you the story "Departing For Heaven."
ANNABELLE:	Oh goodie, goodie, goodie, Aunt Betty. Is the story about Mr. Enoch and Mr. Elijah?
BETTY:	Why, yes, indeed it is. It is the story about these two men that loved God very much, and God loved them very much.
ANNABELLE:	Aunt Betty, that little boy over there is looking at me.
BETTY:	Well, dear me child. Which little boy?
ANNABELLE:	That little cute one that's grinning.
BETTY:	Why dear me, child. All those little boys are grinning and they're all cute. Now if you'll get quiet and still we'll begin our story.
ANNABELLE:	O.K., Aunt Betty, I'm ready.
BETTY:	Our story is right out of the Bible, God's Word. And it's a true story about real people and it happened a long, long time ago.
ANNABELLE:	Longer than a year ago?
BETTY:	Oh dear me, yes. Thousands of years ago.
ANNABELLE:	That sure is a long time ago. That was even before I was born.
BETTY:	Yes, it was, Annabelle. Enoch was a very good man and he loved God very, very much and God loved him very, very much. And the Bible says that he walked with God.
ANNABELLE:	Enoch must have been a good, good man.
BETTY:	Oh, yes he was. I think that Enoch must have been one of the best men living in all the world at that time.
ANNABELLE:	We should all be good and walk with God. Shouldn't we, Aunt Betty?
BETTY:	Yes indeed. That is right, Annabelle. Well, Enoch walked with God and I like to think that everyday God and Enoch would go for a walk and everyday their walk would get longer and longer. And finally one day they walked so far toward God's home that He said to Enoch, "Enoch, we've walked just too far today. Why don't you come on home with

Me today?" For the Bible says God just took Enoch right to Heaven without dying.

ANNABELLE: Oh, Aunt Betty, that was neat!

BETTY: Why yes, child, it was.

ANNABELLE: Was Enoch very old?

BETTY: Well, he was sort of old. He was 365 years old when God took him to Heaven without dying.

ANNABELLE: Wow, Aunt Betty! That's older than *you* are!

BETTY: Yes, it is.

ANNABELLE: Now, Aunt Betty, please tell me about Elijah. Did he go to Heaven without dying too?

BETTY: Yes, indeed he did, child. This is just a wonderful story about Elijah going to Heaven without dying.

ANNABELLE: Oh, Aunt Betty. I'm so excited! Just what happened?

BETTY: Well, our story begins with Elijah getting ready to cross the Jordan River so that he might depart for Heaven. And he had with him his assistant by the name of Elisha. So the story I'm about to tell is true. And the very things that I'm going to tell you were seen by Elisha.

ANNABELLE: Oh goodie, goodie, goodie. I've heard about Elisha. He's the prophet who helped a widow woman pay her husband's bills by selling oil that God had furnished.

BETTY: Why dear me, child. You are smart.

ANNABELLE: Why, thank you, Aunt Betty. I think you are too.

BETTY: Why dear me, little niece. I do believe you're right. Well, let's get along with the story.

ANNABELLE: Oh yes, let's do.

BETTY: As Elijah and Elisha were walking along talking, right out of the sky appeared horses of fire and a chariot of fire and that fiery chariot came right toward Elijah and Elisha.

ANNABELLE: Oh dear me. What on earth happened? Did it run over them?

BETTY: Oh no. It ran right between them and a whirlwind came

21

down and took Elijah straight to Heaven.

ANNABELLE: Oh goodie, goodie. That's neat, too.

BETTY: Yes, Annabelle, it was. That really must have been something to see the chariot and horses. Then Elijah going to Heaven in a whirlwind without dying.

ANNABELLE: Oh, Aunt Betty, this is just so exciting!

BETTY: It certainly is, Annabelle. Being a Christian and serving God is exciting, Annabelle. Did you know that when Jesus comes back to call His church to Heaven that all Christians who are living will go to Heaven without dying?

ANNABELLE: Oh my, Aunt Betty. How exciting that will be!

BETTY: Yes, it will be exciting. That's the reason that it's so important for us to be ready when Jesus comes.

ANNABELLE: You mean to be packed and everything like that?

BETTY: Oh dear me, no child. I mean to be ready to meet Jesus by being a Christian.

ANNABELLE: Oh, you mean by asking Jesus to come into your heart and life.

BETTY: Yes, that's exactly what I mean, Annabelle.

ANNABELLE: Thank you, Aunt Betty, for such an exciting story! I hope that all the boys and girls here will be ready to depart for Heaven when Jesus calls them.

BETTY: Yes, Annabelle, me too. Remember boys and girls, if you've not invited Jesus into your life, today would be a good day to do it.

ANNABELLE: Aunt Betty, when I come back to see you, will you tell me another exciting story?

BETTY: Why yes, Annabelle, I would be delighted to tell you another exciting Bible story. And boys and girls, if you'll come back to Children's Worship I'll tell you an exciting Bible story, too.

ANNABELLE: Good-bye, Aunt Betty.

BETTY: Good-bye, Annabelle and good-bye to you, too, boys and girls. [*Both Puppets exit.*]

FACING THE GIANT

Scripture:	**I Samuel 17:20-54**
Characters:	**2 Puppets, 1 boy and 1 girl**

TAMMY: [*Both puppets appear together.*] Wow! Wow! Wow! They're already here.

SAMMY: Man! I'll say they are! A double wow, wow, wow! Well, hello boys and girls.

TAMMY: Yes, a great big hello.

SAMMY: My name's Sammy and this is my friend Tammy, and we're here today because you're here and we're looking forward to having a good, good, good time.

TAMMY: Yes, boys and girls. We certainly are. Sammy, what is this we're having today?

SAMMY: Why, Tammy, don't tell me you've already forgotten.

TAMMY: No, Sammy, I just wanted to see if you knew.

SAMMY: I sure do. I've already been looking forward to this Children's Worship Rally so that we could be here with all of these beautiful, beautiful, beautiful, I do mean beautiful boys and girls.

TAMMY: Yes, but don't forget all of these beautiful Daddies, too.

SAMMY: Well, I don't know about that. In fact I'm not at all sure about that. But it's good to have all these beautiful Mommies with us.

TAMMY: Oh, Sammy, you're just impossible.

SAMMY: Well, folks, it's good to have all of you here today at our Children's Worship Rally and we're going to have a good, good, good time.

TAMMY: Boy, you can sure say that again, Sammy.

SAMMY: We're going to have a good, good time.

TAMMY: Oh, Sammy, Sammy, Sammy. You are just impossible.

SAMMY: Well, Tammy, what are we going to do for these boys and girls? Would you like for me to sing for them?

TAMMY: Oh gracious, dear me, no. That would be terrible.

SAMMY: And may I ask why it would be so terrible?

TAMMY: Well, the big reason is you couldn't carry a tune in a wash-tub.

SAMMY: Well, I've never thought about that. I guess I could play the piano.

TAMMY: Oh dear me, Sammy. That would even be worse. You can't even play a piano.

SAMMY: Well I know what I can do. I can tell one of my favorite Bible stories.

TAMMY: Oh goodie, goodie, goodie. That you can do, Sammy. You're the best storyteller I know.

SAMMY: What did you say?

TAMMY: I mean you're the best Bible storyteller I know.

SAMMY: Well, that's better. Boys and girls, would you like to hear an exciting story right out of the Bible, God's Holy Word?

TAMMY: I would, too, Sammy. What's it about?

SAMMY: Well, the title of my story is Facing The Giant and it's found in I Samuel. Our story begins with two armies. One on one mountain and one on the other and there was a valley in between them.

TAMMY: Whose armies were they?

SAMMY: Well, they were the armies of the Philistines and the Israel-ites.

TAMMY: Wasn't King Saul the King of Israel?

SAMMY: Yes he was, and he was there with his army.

TAMMY: Did they have a battle?

SAMMY: Well, no they didn't because the Philistines had a big giant on their side. He was over 9 feet tall and his spear weighed over 25 pounds.

TAMMY:	Oh dear me. That was pretty big.
SAMMY:	Man, I'll say. And Saul and the army of Israel were all afraid of him because every day this big giant, by the name of Goliath, would come out on the mountainside and shout out across to the army of Israel and he would say, "Send me a man over here that we might fight."
TAMMY:	Well, what would happen?
SAMMY:	Well, nothing would happen. There wasn't a man in the whole Israelite army who was brave enough to go out and fight with the giant.
TAMMY:	Oh dear, oh dear. What in the world did Saul's army do?
SAMMY:	Well, one day the father of three of Saul's soldiers sent their young brother who was not old enough to be in the army to the place where Israel was camped, with some bread and cheese.
TAMMY:	What was this young brother's name?
SAMMY:	Well, I'm glad you asked that Tammy. His name was David and David arrived at the camp and he went and found his brothers, and while he was talking to them he heard this awful noise.
TAMMY:	What on earth was it? Was it a big bear or some other wild animal?
SAMMY:	Oh dear me, no. It was worse than that. It was the giant Goliath and he was wanting someone to come and fight with him.
TAMMY:	Did David run back home when he heard the giant?
SAMMY:	Oh dear me, no. David wanted to know why someone didn't go and fight with him. And the men told him that everyone was afraid of the giant.
TAMMY:	Then did he run home?
SAMMY:	Oh no, not David. He said, "If no one else will go and fight with the giant, I will."
TAMMY:	Why, how could he fight with the giant? I thought you said he was just a boy.
SAMMY:	Well, that's what everyone else asked, too. But do you know

what David told them?

TAMMY: No, what did he tell them?

SAMMY: Well, David told them that while he was keeping his father's sheep — you see David was a shepherd — a bear and a lion came out to get the sheep and David grabbed that lion by the beard . . . .

TAMMY: Well, that was neat! I bet that lion hollered!

SAMMY: It did more than that. David killed the lion and the bear.

TAMMY: You mean all by himself?

SAMMY: No, not exactly. You see the Lord was with him and helped him to kill the lion and bear.

TAMMY: Oh isn't that wonderful! God always helps us when we need Him, doesn't He Sammy?

SAMMY: Yes, Tammy. He really does. And boys and girls, He will always help you if you'll just ask Him to.

TAMMY: Well, what happened next? Did David go out and fight with the giant?

SAMMY: No, King Saul came out and wanted David to wear all of his armor.

TAMMY: Well, wasn't it a little big?

SAMMY: Man! It sure was! David sure was funny looking. The helmet came down over his eyes and the coat dragged on the ground. David took it off and said, "This just will never do."

TAMMY: Then what happened?

SAMMY: Well, David said to King Saul, "I just can't wear all of this armor. I've got to just be me."

TAMMY: Well, we can never be anyone but ourselves, can we, Sammy.

SAMMY: No, Tammy, we can't. Boys and girls, never try to be someone you're not. Just be yourself and let God use you.

TAMMY: Well, how did God use David?

SAMMY: Well, David took his staff in his hand and as he crossed the little brook to go meet the giant, he reached down and picked up five smooth stones. And he put them in his shepherd's bag, and he took with him his slingshot.

TAMMY: Oh, mercy me. You mean David didn't have a sword?

SAMMY: No, indeed. All he had was a slingshot and his little stones. And when Goliath saw him coming he just went into a rage.

TAMMY: Why did he get so mad?

SAMMY: Well, the reason he got mad was because he saw David coming and David was just a boy. But he didn't know that God was with David. The giant shouted at David, "Come on over here little boy. I'm going to feed you to the birds today."

TAMMY: Oh dear me. Oh mercy, dear me. Oh my, oh me, oh dear me. I think I may faint.

SAMMY: Oh Tammy, you always say you're going to faint. There's nothing to worry about. God was with David.

TAMMY: Well please, quick hurry. Tell us what happened. I want to know. Don't you boys and girls want to know?

SAMMY: Well, if you'll quit interrupting me, Tammy, I'll finish the story.

TAMMY: Oh, I'm sorry.

SAMMY: Goliath the giant started toward David. David put a smooth stone in his slingshot and began to whirl it around as he ran toward the giant, and at the right time the stone came out and hit the giant between the eyes . . . .

TAMMY: Oh dear!

SAMMY: And the giant fell down flat on his face and the ground trembled. Then David ran up, grabbed the giant's own sword and cut off his head.

TAMMY: Oh me. Dear me. I feel sick. Oh I am sick. Oh, I'm going to faint. [*She faints.*]

SAMMY: Man, oh, man! She really meant it this time. Tammy, Tammy, get up, get up.

TAMMY: Oh, oh, where am I? What happened?

SAMMY:	You're here at Children's Worship Rally and I've been telling the story about facing the giant and when I came to the part about David facing the giant and cutting . . .
TAMMY:	Oh dear, oh dear. I remember now. Please don't say it again.
SAMMY:	O.K. Tammy, I won't mention it again about David cutting off his head.
TAMMY:	Oh dear, oh dear. I do believe I'm going to be sick again.
SAMMY:	Here we go again. Now Tammy, get a hold of yourself so I can finish the story.
TAMMY:	O.K., O.K. I'm going to be all right. Please go on.
SAMMY:	Well, after David slew Goliath, the Philistines started running away and everyone knew about the God of Israel, David's God. Boys and girls, it took a lot of courage for David to face the giant.
TAMMY:	But David knew that God was on his side all the time.
SAMMY:	Yes, he did Tammy. And boys and girls if you know Jesus as your Saviour, you too can face the giants and He will help you slay them.
TAMMY:	What kind of giants do we have today, Sammy?
SAMMY:	Well, we have the giant of lying, the giant of stealing, the giant of cheating, the giant of disobedience. But with God's help, we can slay them all.
TAMMY:	Oh, that is so wonderful, Sammy, and it's so true for Jesus said, "I will be with you always."
SAMMY:	Well, boys and girls, did you enjoy the story? I'm glad you did. Now remember, be strong like David and trust in the Lord and you can face the giants.
TAMMY:	Yes, boys and girls. Always love Jesus and serve Him.
SAMMY:	See you at Children's Worship boys and girls.
TAMMY:	Yes, and don't be late.
TOGETHER:	Good-bye and God bless each of you. [*Both Puppets exit.*]

FIRE FROM HEAVEN

Scripture:	**I Kings 18:17-40**
Characters:	**2 Puppets, 1 boy and 1 girl (both young)**

SONNY: [*Both puppets appear together.*] Honey, it sure is good to be back again at Children's Worship, isn't it?

HONEY: Why yes, it really is, I have really missed all of the boys and girls.

TOGETHER: Good morning, boys and girls.

HONEY: It's just so much fun being here at Children's Worship with all these boys and girls.

SONNY: Why yes, Honey, it is so wonderful that we can come and worship the Lord. God has really blessed kids here in this country.

HONEY: Why my, oh me, He really has. Boys and girls in other parts of the world cannot come to church and worship God like we can.

SONNY: That certainly is right, Honey. Did you know that people worship some strange things?

HONEY: Why yes, yes. Dear me, yes, yes. Why in India people worship cows.

SONNY: Yes, and in other parts of the world they worship rocks and trees and great big statues.

HONEY: Oh dear me, Sonny. It is just so sad that people worship such false gods.

SONNY: Why, yes indeed it is, for the Bible says that there is only one God and that everyone should worship Him.

HONEY: Sonny, doesn't the Bible tell us about what happened when people worshiped these false gods?

SONNY: Well, I'm just so glad you asked that question, Honey. Yes, the Bible does have something to say about worshiping false gods.

HONEY: Sonny, I can see that look in your eye. I do believe that you have a Bible story that you want to share with the boys and girls.

SONNY: Well, now that you mentioned it, Honey, I believe that I do and it's all about the power of God over the false teaching of idol worshipers.

HONEY: What's an idol? One of those great big statues?

SONNY: Yes, indeedy, deed, deed. That is correct, correct.

HONEY: Well, what is the title of the story and where is it found in the Bible?

SONNY: Well, the title of the story is "Fire From Heaven" and it is found in I Kings the eighteenth chapter.

HONEY: Oh my, oh my, oh my. Oh me, oh me, oh my. That sounds so exciting.

SONNY: Why yes indeed, it is. Our story begins with a meeting between the wicked King of Israel and the prophet of God.

HONEY: What were their names?

SONNY: The wicked King's name was Ahab and the prophet of God's name was Elijah. When Elijah met Ahab he said to him, "You wicked king. You have forsaken the commandments of God and are following Baal."

HONEY: Oh dear, oh dear. How terrible, terrible, terrible. Who in the world was Baal?

SONNY: Baal was a false god. Now Elijah was going to prove to the people that Baal was not really a god at all.

HONEY: Oh my, oh my, oh me. How was he going to do that?

SONNY: Well, Elijah said to Ahab, "Let's get all the people together and meet on the mountain by the name of Carmel."

HONEY: Well, that sounds like something to eat.

SONNY: Oh Honey, you're just impossible. Now where was I? Oh yes, Elijah wanted all the men of Israel and all the prophets of Baal to meet up on Mt. Carmel.

HONEY: Were there many evil prophets of Baal?

SONNY: Why, yes there were. In fact there were 850 of them.

HONEY:	Wow! Wow! Wow! Was Elijah the only prophet of God there? Was he all alone? Huh, huh?
SONNY:	Well yes, he was the only prophet of God there but he was sure not alone because God was with him.
HONEY:	What in the world did Elijah do up there on that mountain?
SONNY:	Well, he said to the people, "I want you to decide today who will be your god. Will it be Baal or will the Lord be God?"
HONEY:	Well what did they say?
SONNY:	Dear me. They didn't say anything. So Elijah said to them, "All right, let's build two altars. One to Baal and one to God. And we will put wood on the altars and I will take a bull and you will take a bull and we will cut them to pieces and place them on the altars, but we will not put any fire under them."
HONEY:	Goodness me, goodness me, goodness me. What did Elijah do all of that for? How could they have a sacrifice if they had no fire to burn it up?
SONNY:	Man alive, Honey. This is the exciting part about the story. Elijah said to the priests of Baal, "All right boys, you pray and have your god send down fire from Heaven and burn up your altar."
HONEY:	Oh dear, oh dear, oh dear. I'm just so excited. What happened?
SONNY:	Well, from morning until noontime the prophets of Baal cried and prayed to Baal but there was no answer. Why they even leaped up and down on top of the altar.
HONEY:	Why dear me. That must have been a strange sight to see all of those men jumping up and down.
SONNY:	Oh me, that's not all they did. They even cut themselves with knives until they were just bleeding all over.
HONEY:	Oh dear me, oh dear me. I think I'm going to faint.
SONNY:	Oh you girls. A little blood's not going to hurt anything.
HONEY:	Oh dear, oh dear, oh dear. I'm getting sick, sick, sick.
SONNY:	O.K., O.K. I won't say anything else about the blood running all over the place.

HONEY:	Oh, oh, oh. I know I'm going to faint.
SONNY:	Sorry.
HONEY:	Gulp, gulp, what, what. What happened next?
SONNY:	Well, they carried on all day like this and their god never did answer. So Elijah fixed up his altar and placed his sacrifice on it.
HONEY:	Then did he pray and did God send fire down from Heaven?
SONNY:	Well no, Honey. He didn't. The next thing he did was dig a little trench.
HONEY:	What in the world is a trench?
SONNY:	Gracious, Honey, don't you know anything? That's a hole all the way around the altar.
HONEY:	Why on earth would he do a thing like that?
SONNY:	Well, the next thing he did was throw four barrels of water right over the sacrifice and it ran over the sacrifice and the altar and it filled up the trench.
HONEY:	Wow! Then he prayed and fire came down from Heaven.
SONNY:	Well no, not yet. Elijah had them pour four more barrels of water on the altar.
HONEY:	My, my. Things must have really been wet. Then did he pray and did fire come down from Heaven?
SONNY:	I'm afraid not, Honey, not yet. He poured four more barrels of water on.
HONEY:	Oh my, oh my, oh my. Things really were wet.
SONNY:	Man, I'll say they were. Then Elijah stepped up to the altar and he prayed to the God of Heaven, the only true God.
HONEY:	Oh dear, oh dear. How exciting! How exciting! What happened next? Did the fire fall from Heaven?
SONNY:	Boy! I'll say. After Elijah prayed the fire of the Lord fell and burned up the sacrifice, the wood and the stones and even the dust and all the water that was in the trench.
HONEY:	Oh dear, oh dear, oh dear. How wonderful, how wonderful,

how wonderful. Then did the people believe in God?

SONNY: Yes, Honey, they did. They believed in God.

HONEY: Oh how wonderful God is, and He loves us so much.

SONNY: Yes Honey, God really loves us, and boys and girls, God loves you too. He loves you so much that He sent His Son Jesus to die on the cross for all of your sins.

HONEY: Yes boys and girls. He did send Jesus to die just for you. Sonny, do you remember that verse in the Bible about Jesus knocking at the door of our lives, wanting in?

SONNY: Why yes, indeed I do, Honey. That verse is found in Revelation Chapter 3 verse 20.

HONEY: Would you quote it for the boys and girls?

SONNY: Why, I would be delighted to. Here it is: "Behold, I stand at the door, and knock: if any man hear my voice, and open the door, I will come in to him, and will sup with him, and he with me." Boys and girls, if Jesus is knocking at your door today, won't you let Him come in?

HONEY: Oh Sonny, I just wish that I was a people so that Jesus would knock at my heart's door.

SONNY: Oh, that would be wonderful, but Jesus only knocks at the door of people's hearts.

HONEY: Well, Sonny, I guess we had better be going.

SONNY: Yep, I guess you're right.

TOGETHER: Boys and girls remember, God loves you. We will see you again soon. Good-bye. [*Both Puppets exit.*]

WHEN LITTLE BECAME MUCH

Scripture: II Kings 4:1-7
Characters: 2 Puppets, 1 boy and 1 girl

TOGETHER: [*Both puppets come onstage together.*] Good morning boys and girls.

HONEY: Boys and girls, I have missed you and I know Sonny has too.

SONNY: Well, yes indeed, Honey. I have missed all of these wonderful boys and girls. It's just so good to be back at Children's Worship.

HONEY: Boys and girls, I wonder if you would like to sing a couple of songs with Sonny and me. God has done so much for us and He loves us so that I just want to sing about how good He is.

SONNY: Yes, Honey, God is good and He just loves us so. In fact, our Pastor preached a sermon about God loving donkeys and even worms. So I know He loves me.

HONEY: My, oh me, oh me. I know that God loves donkeys and that He loves me but I've never thought about worms. They're so wriggly and slimy. Oh, I think I'm going to be sick. Oh me, oh me, oh me.

SONNY: Oh, Honey, don't be silly. Worms never hurt anyone. Besides birds and fishes like them.

HONEY: Well, I'm not a bird or a fish. I'm a people puppet and I don't like worms.

SONNY: Honey, let's get back to our singing. What are we going to sing with the boys and girls?

HONEY: Well, let's sing "God Is So Good." All of you boys and girls must know that song. All right boys and girls, together now. Let's all sing.

SONNY: Honey, you know that song reminds me of a story that I heard in Sunday School. I wonder if the boys and girls would like to hear it.

HONEY: Why yes, Sonny, I think they would. What is the story all about?

SONNY: Well, the title of the story is "When Little Became Much" and it's about Elisha and a poor widow woman.

HONEY: Oh Sonny, I think that would be an exciting story. We won't even sing another song if you'll tell us the story right now.

SONNY: Well, if you insist and really want to hear it.

HONEY: Oh I do, I do, I do. Really I do, I do, I do. I want to hear it just from you, I do.

SONNY: And what about *you* boys and girls? Do you want to hear the story "When Little Became Much?"

HONEY: Well, what are you waiting for?

SONNY: Well, nothing. Our story took place a long time ago and if you wanted to read about it in the Bible you could find it in II Kings chapter four, verses one through seven.

HONEY: Second Kings is in the Old Testament, isn't it?

SONNY: Why, yes it is, Honey. Our story begins one day with a woman coming to see Elisha the prophet and she had a real big problem.

HONEY: You mean a real, big problem? Even bigger than the one you got into when you tried to sleep with the goldfish, and the water all spilled out in the bed and you had a bed full of gold-fish and water?

SONNY: My yes. That was a big problem but this woman's problem was even bigger than that. Her husband had died and she had no money, and some people that she owed money to were going to take her two sons and make slaves out of them.

HONEY: Wow! Wow! Wow! Oh me, my! Jumping bullfrogs! That was a problem. What did Elisha do? Loan her some money?

SONNY: No, no, no. Elisha asked her what she had in her house.

HONEY: Well, what in the world did he ask her a question like that for?

SONNY: Well, if you would just keep from interrupting me so much, I could tell you.

HONEY: Sorry.

SONNY: Well, the woman thought for a minute and she said, "Mr. Elisha, I don't have anything in my house except just a

35

little pot of oil."

HONEY: Oh, dear me. Oh, dear me. She really was a poor widow woman with just one pot of oil.

SONNY: Yes, Honey, she was a poor widow woman. But God was with her and He loved her very much.

HONEY: Well, what did Elisha do next?

SONNY: Well, he told this woman to send her sons to all the neighbors and borrow all the pots and pans and jars that they could possibly borrow that were empty, and to bring them to her and then shut the door.

HONEY: Boy! That sure seemed like a dumb thing to do. What was she going to do with all of those empty pots and pans and jars?

SONNY: Well, Honey, it certainly wasn't dumb because Elisha had a plan.

HONEY: What was the plan?

SONNY: Well, Elisha told the widow woman to take her little pot of oil and to fill all the pots and pans and jars that she had borrowed.

HONEY: Gracious, gracious. That would be a miracle to take one little pot of oil and fill all of those empty ones. But God can do it.

SONNY: Yes, Honey. God did do it. She kept pouring and pouring and pouring until there wasn't an empty pot or pan or jar in the whole house. Then after she had filled up all of the empty vessels, Elisha told her to go and sell the oil and pay her bills and then she could live on the rest of the money.

HONEY: Wow! God is really good, and when we let God take care of us even the little we have can become much.

SONNY: Yes, Honey, that's true. God really loved that woman and her two sons. And boys and girls, He wants to love you just like that.

HONEY: Why, yes He does, boys and girls. God loves each of you just as much as He loved that poor widow woman.

SONNY: That's the reason God wants us to be good, isn't it, Honey?

HONEY: Why, yes it is. God wants us to love Him, and to serve Him.

SONNY: You know, Honey, I remember a Bible verse that I learned in Sunday School. It's John three, three, three . . .

HONEY: You mean John 3:16?

SONNY: Why yes, Honey, that's it. John 3:16. Will you help me say it?

HONEY: Why yes, I would be glad, glad, glad to.

TOGETHER: "For God so loved the world, that he gave his only begotten Son, that whosoever believeth in him should not perish, but have everlasting life."

SONNY: Well, boys and girls, God really loves you and even if you are little He wants you to become much for Him. Well, Honey, we'd better go for today. It won't be long before lunch time and boy am I hungry!

HONEY: I'm hungry too, Sonny. But I'm also happy because I know God loves me and He cares for me just like that little widow woman.

TOGETHER: Good-bye, boys and girls. See you real soon. [*Both Puppets exit.*]

WHEN THE SUN BACKED UP

Scripture: II Kings 20:1-11
Characters: 2 Puppets, 1 boy and 1 girl

GRUMPY HERMAN: [*Grumpy Herman comes onstage.*] Oh, I feel terrible. I do believe I'm sick. Oh, I know I'm sick. In fact I think I may die. Oh me, how terrible.

SAMMY: [*Sammy comes onstage.*] What in the world is all this commotion? I've never heard such complaining in all my life. Oh, oh, I might have known. It's you, Grumpy Herman. Why are you so grumpy all the time?

GRUMPY HERMAN: You'd be grumpy too if you were dying.

SAMMY: You don't look like you're dying to me. In fact you look very much alive. In fact you look disgustingly healthy.

GRUMPY HERMAN: Well, I feel just terrible.

SAMMY: Well, where do you hurt? Your head, stomach . . .

GRUMPY HERMAN: Well all over. And nobody cares. I mean nobody cares.

SAMMY: Oh dear me, Grumpy Herman, if you wouldn't be so grumpy you wouldn't feel so bad. And somebody does love you.

GRUMPY HERMAN: Well, I would sure like to know who. Just tell me who loves me.

SAMMY: Well, Grumpy Herman, I love you.

GRUMPY HERMAN: You do? What do you want to borrow, Sammy?

SAMMY: Why, Grumpy, I don't want to borrow a thing. I really do love you. And Tammy loves you. And Betty and Freddie. Yes and even little Annabelle. Then there's Sonny and Honey and Aunt Suzie and Uncle Dandy. They all love you.

GRUMPY HERMAN: Anybody else?

SAMMY: Why yes. All of these boys and girls do.

GRUMPY HERMAN: They do?

SAMMY: But most of all God loves you, Grumpy Herman.

GRUMPY HERMAN: Sammy, you mean God really cares about me?

SAMMY: Yes, God really cares about you. God loves everyone. He even knows how many hairs we have on our head.

GRUMPY HERMAN: Wow! Wow! Wow! You mean God knows how many hairs I have on my head?

SAMMY: He sure does, Grumpy.

GRUMPY HERMAN: Wow! Can you imagine! With hair like mine!

SAMMY: Yes, even with a hairdo like yours, Grumpy Herman. He even sees the little sparrow when it falls to the ground dead.

GRUMPY HERMAN: Oh dear me. I'd better quit shooting at little sparrows. Sammy, God knows everything, doesn't He?

SAMMY: Yes, indeed He does.

GRUMPY HERMAN: Does He even care when you're sick and even dying like I am? Oh, oh, oh.

SAMMY: Oh, Grumpy Herman, stop that. You're not dying. And yes, God is concerned about anyone that is sick.

GRUMPY HERMAN: Well, how do you know?

SAMMY: Well, the Bible tells me so. In fact, Grumpy Herman, I know a story right out of the Bible, God's Holy Word. And the title of it is "When The Sun Backed Up."

GRUMPY HERMAN: When whose son backed up? When, where, why?

SAMMY: Oh dear me, Grumpy, I'm not talking about somebody's son. I'm talking about the sun up in the sky that shines.

GRUMPY HERMAN: Well, how could the sun do that? All I've ever seen it do is come up and go down. I've never seen it back up. Does the Bible really say that?

SAMMY: Yes, it does. In II Kings 20:1-11. Do you want to hear about it?

GRUMPY HERMAN: Man! I sure do. I really do. I positively do.

SAMMY: Well, our story begins with a King by the name of Hezekiah . . . .

GRUMPY HERMAN: Heze . . . who?

SAMMY: With King Hezekiah.

GRUMPY HERMAN: That sure is a peculiar name.

SAMMY: Well, Grumpy Herman is a pretty peculiar name to me.

GRUMPY HERMAN: On with the story please.

SAMMY: Well, King Hezekiah was very, very sick and God sent the Prophet Isaiah to tell King Hezekiah that he was going to die.

GRUMPY HERMAN: Oh dear me. What did the poor fellow do?

SAMMY: What did who do?

GRUMPY HERMAN: What did the King do?

SAMMY: Well, the Bible says that he turned his face to the wall and he began to cry.

GRUMPY HERMAN: Wow! I don't blame him. I even feel like crying now. Then what happened?

SAMMY: Well, not only did King Hezekiah cry but he began to pray, and he asked the Lord to help him in his time of need.

GRUMPY HERMAN: Did God really hear him?

SAMMY: He sure did.

GRUMPY HERMAN: Dear me. What happened next?

SAMMY: Well, before Isaiah the Prophet could leave the King's house, God spoke to Isaiah.

GRUMPY HERMAN: Oh my, how exciting! What did He say to him?

SAMMY: Well, God said to Isaiah, "Go back up to King Hezekiah's room and tell him I've heard his prayers and I've seen his tears and I'm going to heal him of his sickness."

GRUMPY HERMAN: My, how exciting!

SAMMY: Yes, it is exciting. Not only was God going to heal King Hezekiah, but He told him He was going to let him live for 15 more years.

GRUMPY HERMAN: Man alive! That was really something. How did God go about healing him?

SAMMY: Well, God told Isaiah to tell King Hezekiah's servants to take a lump of figs and to lay it on the boil that was causing all of his sickness.

GRUMPY HERMAN: Do you mean it really worked?

SAMMY: It sure did, for the Bible says that King Hezekiah recovered.

GRUMPY HERMAN: Wow, wow, wow! I'd better get me some figs. Well, what did the King say about all of this?

SAMMY: King Hezekiah asked the Prophet Isaiah for a sign that God was going to heal him.

GRUMPY HERMAN: For a sign? What kind of sign? Do you mean a sign like along the road?

SAMMY: Oh dear me no, Grumpy Herman. If you just wouldn't be so grumpy all the time and read the Bible more and go to Sunday School you would know about some of these things.

GRUMPY HERMAN: I guess you're right, Sammy. I'm going to start doing better. Did God give King Hezekiah a sign?

SAMMY: He sure did. Isaiah said to King Hezekiah, "What do you want the Lord to do for you? Shall the sun go down 10° or go back 10°?"

GRUMPY HERMAN: Well, which did the King want to happen?

SAMMY: King Hezekiah said, "I want the sun to back up."

GRUMPY HERMAN: Wow! I've never heard of that before.

SAMMY: Neither had the King. But when the Prophet Isaiah prayed and asked God to back up the sun that's exactly what happened, the sun backed up.

GRUMPY HERMAN: Sammy, God is really wonderful, isn't He? King Hezekiah got well and the sun backed up. Oh how wonderful God is.

SAMMY: Yes, God is wonderful. And He loves and He cares for us all.

GRUMPY HERMAN: You know something, Sammy? I don't feel sick anymore. In fact after hearing this story, I don't even feel grumpy. I believe that God loves even me.

SAMMY: Right you are. And boys and girls, God loves even you.

GRUMPY HERMAN: Come on, Sammy, we'd better hurry or we'll be late.

SAMMY: Late for what?

GRUMPY HERMAN: Why, late for church. I want to hear more about God's love
                for me.

SAMMY: Wow! Grumpy Herman, you sure are a changed person. I'm
                ready to go. [*Both Puppets exit.*]

WHEN IT'S COOL IN THE FURNACE

Scripture:	**Daniel 3**
Characters:	**2 Puppets, 1 boy and 1 girl**

FREDDIE: [*Freddie comes out looking around.*] Man! I sure hope I get one. In fact, I hope I get several. I would really like to get a lot.

BETTY: [*Comes up behind Freddie while he's talking.*] Freddie, what would you like to get a lot of?

FREDDIE: [*Jumps*] Wow! You almost scared me to death. What do you mean sneaking up behind me like that?

BETTY: Oh, Freddie. You are as jumpy as a long-tailed cat in a roomful of rocking chairs. Now tell me, what is it you want a lot of?

FREDDIE: Well, Betty, don't you know what February the 14th is?

BETTY: Oh dear me. I do believe, yes I do know, why I'm even certain . . .

FREDDIE: Yep, yep, yep. You're right, right. It's Valentine's Day. And I want to get a lot of valentines.

BETTY: Well, well, Freddie. Do you think anyone loves you enough to send you a lot of valentines?

FREDDIE: Man alive! I hadn't thought about that. But you know, Betty, I believe that all these boys and girls love me. Don't you boys and girls? And Betty, don't you love me too?

BETTY: Why yes, Freddie. I sure do. We should all love each other. Freddie, are you going to send me a valentine?

FREDDIE: Well, Betty, I sure am. And if I wasn't a puppet I'd send all of these boys and girls one too.

BETTY: Oh, how nice that would be. I'm glad that you love me, Freddie.

FREDDIE: Well, my, my, my, my, Betty. We Christians are supposed to love each other because God loves us.

BETTY: Yes, Freddie, I know He does. For the Bible tells us that God loves all boys and girls in all the world.

FREDDIE:	Yes, that is true. Just the other day I was reading a story right out of the Bible, God's Book.
BETTY:	What was it about, Freddie? Huh? What was it about, huh, huh?
FREDDIE:	Well, if you'll just calm down and give me a chance. The story was about "When It's Cool In The Furnace."
BETTY:	Oh Freddie, Freddie, Freddie. I just can't wait to hear about when the furnace gets cold.
FREDDIE:	Oh dear me, Betty. You're already confused. Just let me start from the very beginning with this exciting story from the Bible, God's Holy Word.
BETTY:	Oh yes, yes. Please do. Oops, sorry.
FREDDIE:	Our story takes place in a land called Babylon and the story is about three young men by the names of Hananiah, Mishael, and Azariah. And, oh yes, there was a king by the name of Nebuchadnezzar.
BETTY:	Oh me, my. What a peculiar name. Did you say the king's name was Nebuchadnebber?
FREDDIE:	Why no, Betty. It's Nebuchadnezzar. But it is a strange name. And oh yes, the king changed the names of Hananiah, Mishael, and Azariah to Shadrach, Meshach, and Abed-nego.
BETTY:	Oh yes, I know all about Shadrach, Meshach, and Abed-nego. They were three young Jewish boys.
FREDDIE:	Yes, they were, Betty. Now if you will just please quit interrupting me, I'll get along with the story.
BETTY:	Sorry!
FREDDIE:	King Nebuchadnezzar made a great big statue out of gold and it was ninety feet high and nine feet wide.
BETTY:	Wow! Wow! I do mean wow, wow! That was a big thing. It was as big as a tree.
FREDDIE:	Yes, I guess it must have been and it was tall, too. Well King Nebuchadnezzar sent a message to all of the princes, governors, captains, judges, treasurers, counselors, sheriffs and all of his rulers to come and see the statue that he had made.

BETTY:	Man, oh man! That was a lot of people. Did they come?
FREDDIE:	They sure did. And when they had all arrived, one of the King's men said to them, "When the band begins to play, the King wants everyone to fall down on his face and worship the statue. And if you don't, the King will have you thrown into the fiery furnace."
BETTY:	Wow! That was something! In fact, that was terrible!
FREDDIE:	It was even hot, too.
BETTY:	Well, what happened? Did everyone bow down? Did Shadrach, Meshach and Abed-nego?
FREDDIE:	Oh no. They were God's men and the King wanted them to worship that statue but they could only worship the true God.
BETTY:	Well, what in the world happened?
FREDDIE:	Well, when the King heard about Shadrach, Meshach, and Abed-nego not bowing down to his statue, he got so excited his face turned red. Then he began to shout and scream and had them brought before him.
BETTY:	Boy! Things were really hot for them.
FREDDIE:	You can say that again, Betty.
BETTY:	Boy! Things were really hot for them.
FREDDIE:	Betty, will you quit interrupting me?
BETTY:	But you said . . .
FREDDIE:	Betty, if you don't quit interrupting me, I'll never get through with this story. King Nebuchadnezzar said to Shadrach, Meshach, and Abed-nego, "Boys, I'm going to give you one more chance. When you hear the music, fall down and worship my golden image or I'm going to throw you into the furnace."
BETTY:	Oh dear me, oh dear me, oh dear me. I'm just so excited. What happened, what happened, what happened?
FREDDIE:	Well, they looked at the King, eyeball to eyeball, and said, "King, we just can't do it. We love God too much and He loves us." Boy! That did it.

BETTY:	Oh my goodness. Did what?
FREDDIE:	Why, it got them thrown right into that fiery furnace. The King had them heat the furnace seven times hotter than it had ever been heated, and he called for the strongest men anywhere around and these men grabbed Shadrach, Meshach, and Abed-nego and tied them up and threw them into the furnace.
BETTY:	Oh dear me. I think I may faint. How hot did you say that furnace was?
FREDDIE:	It was seven times hotter than usual. It was so hot that the flames just leaped out and killed the strong men when they threw Shadrach, Meshach, and Abed-nego into the furnace.
BETTY:	Oh, Freddie. How terrible, how terrible. How horrible, how horrible.
FREDDIE:	Yeah, it was pretty bad.
BETTY:	I thought you said that this was a story about being cool in the furnace. It sure doesn't seem very cool.
FREDDIE:	Well now, Betty, it was only cool for God's three men because God was with Shadrach, Meshach, and Abed-nego. For the King came close to the furnace and he looked in, and man, was he ever surprised. Instead of three being in there, he saw four men in that furnace.
BETTY:	Oh Freddie. Wasn't that wonderful! God must have sent a messenger from Heaven to help Shadrach, Meshach and Abed-nego. Now I can see that it was cool in the furnace.
FREDDIE:	Yes, Betty, it sure was. God was with them because He loved them and they loved Him and wanted to serve Him.
BETTY:	God sent Shadrach, Meshach and Abed-nego a big valentine that said "I love you."
FREDDIE:	Well, Betty, I guess you could say that. But God sent His Son Jesus to die on the cross for all of us because He loves us.
BETTY:	I sure wish I wasn't a puppet so I could give my heart to Jesus.
FREDDIE:	Yes, Betty, me too. But only real people can give their hearts to Jesus.
BETTY:	Is that all of the story?

FREDDIE:	Well no, Betty, it sure isn't. King Nebuchadnezzar called down to Shadrach, Meshach and Abed-nego and said, "Boys, come on out." And they just stepped right up out of the furnace. And the King said to them, "Boys, I believe in your God and I'd better not hear anyone say a thing against Him or I'll have them torn in two."
BETTY:	Oh dear, oh dear. That would be enough to tear you up.
FREDDIE:	Man, I'll say! Then the King promoted Shadrach, Meshach and Abed-nego.
BETTY:	It really pays to serve God.
FREDDIE:	Yes, Betty, it really does. We should all love God like Shadrach, Meshach, and Abed-nego. You know Betty, God really loves us all.
BETTY:	Yes, Freddie. He really does for the Bible tells us so, and boys and girls, He loves you.
FREDDIE:	Betty, uh, uh, are you . . . I mean . . .
BETTY:	Dear me, dear me, what do you want to know?
FREDDIE:	Will you be my Abed-nego . . . I mean Shadrach . . . oh dear, what do I mean?
BETTY:	Freddie, do you want me to be your Valentine?
FREDDIE:	Oh wow! Wow! Wow! Seventy times wow! That's just exactly what I mean.
BETTY:	Oh yes, Freddie. I would be most, most, most happy to be your Valentine.
FREDDIE:	Oh, I'm so happy, happy, happy, happy and I'm glad too. Boys and girls, won't you be a valentine for Jesus and say "I love you" to Him?
BETTY:	Yes, boys and girls, when you love and serve Jesus, it is always . . .
TOGETHER:	COOL IN THE FURNACE! Bye-bye. [*Both Puppets exit.*]

WHEN THE LIONS REFUSED TO EAT

Scripture:	**Daniel 6**
Characters:	**2 Puppets, 1 man and 1 woman (both elderly)**

UNCLE DANDY: [*Both puppets come onstage together.*] Good morning boys and girls. My name is Uncle Dandy and I want to introduce you to Aunt Suzie.

AUNT SUZIE: Well, hello there boys and girls. It's just so good to see you here today at Children's Worship. Uncle Dandy, this is just about the finest looking group of boys and girls I think I have ever seen. Don't you think so?

UNCLE DANDY: Why yes, Aunt Suzie. It surely is. Boys and girls, Aunt Suzie and Uncle Dandy have heard so much about you from Sonny and Honey. They've been telling us what good boys and girls you are. So now we're looking forward to sharing with you some wonderful stories.

AUNT SUZIE: Yes, Uncle Dandy, we really are. But before our story today, I would like to ask the boys and girls what Sunday this is. Boys and girls, who can be the first to tell me what Sunday this is? [*Pause*] That's right. This is the first Sunday of a New Year.

UNCLE DANDY: Aunt Suzie, I'm always excited about a New Year. There are so many wonderful things that can happen to us in this coming year.

AUNT SUZIE: Yes, Uncle Dandy, there are just so many, many things. I hope that each boy and girl here today that is not a Christian will let Jesus come into his heart during the New Year.

UNCLE DANDY: Yes, that would be wonderful. That would be better than falling in a barrel of honey. And wouldn't it be wonderful if all of these beautiful children would try to be in Sunday School every single Sunday during this New Year?

AUNT SUZIE: Why, Uncle Dandy, what a dandy, dandy idea! And not only attend Sunday School every Sunday, but Children's Worship, too!

UNCLE DANDY: Wow, wow, wow! Wouldn't that be just something. Aunt Suzie, get ready; I want you to count the hands. Boys and girls, if you will do your best to be in Sunday School and Children's Worship every Sunday unless you are sick or out of town, put your hand up high. Real high now.

AUNT SUZIE:	Well, Uncle Dandy, look at all those hands. My, won't this be wonderful!
UNCLE DANDY:	Yes, it will. I know that the Lord Jesus will be pleased. O.K., boys and girls, you can put your hands down.
AUNT SUZIE:	Uncle Dandy, are you ready for our Bible Story today?
UNCLE DANDY:	Yes, I think we are and this is an exciting story entitled "When The Lions Refused To Eat."
AUNT SUZIE:	My, Uncle Dandy, that sounds like an exciting story.
UNCLE DANDY:	Yes, Aunt Suzie, it's very exciting. But it's a very true story. Our story took place a long time ago when there were kings and princes. The king's name in our story was King Darius. He was a good king but he did not serve God as he should. Now King Darius chose 120 princes to help him rule over the land.
AUNT SUZIE:	My, that was a lot of men to help him rule.
UNCLE DANDY:	Yes, Aunt Suzie, it was, but it was a large kingdom. And over these 120 princes the King chose three presidents. And a young man by the name of Daniel was chosen to be the first. Daniel was a young man who loved God very, very much and in everything that Daniel did he tried to please God. The King could trust Daniel. Daniel always told the truth. He didn't steal. He didn't say naughty words.
AUNT SUZIE:	Uncle Dandy, this is the way we should all live if we're Christians, isn't it?
UNCLE DANDY:	Why, yes it is, Aunt Suzie. Each of us should try to live like Daniel and please the Lord Jesus. Boys and girls, do you always tell the truth and obey your parents and use nice talk? I sure hope so for I would like for each of you to be a Daniel. But boys and girls, not everyone liked Daniel. The other presidents and princes were very, very, very; oh they were just very, very, very . . .
AUNT SUZIE:	Uncle Dandy, you mean they were very, very, very . . .
UNCLE DANDY:	Oh me, oh my, yes. I do mean they were most, most, very, very, very *jealous* of Daniel because he loved and served his God.
AUNT SUZIE:	Well, gracious me, oh my. What in the world did they do about it?

UNCLE DANDY: Well, they went to see the King and they said, "Oh, oh, oh, oh, King Darius live forever, and ever." And boy, did this make the King feel good! He began to swell up like a big fat toadfrog. And he said, "Boys, what is on your mind?" "All the presidents, the governors, the princes, the counselors and the captains have gotten together," they said. "And we would like, O King, for you to make it a law that for 30 days all people must pray to no other man or god but to you only, King Darius. And if they do, they'll be thrown in the lions' den."

AUNT SUZIE: Oh gracious me, oh my, oh my, oh me, oh my. How dreadful, how dreadful, how dreadful, dreadful. Oh, how dreadful, dreadful!

UNCLE DANDY: Yes, indeed. That was dreadful, dreadful, dreadful. In fact, it was just bad. It was even worse than bad. It was terrible!

AUNT SUZIE: Well, Uncle Dandy, what happened next? This is just so exciting!

UNCLE DANDY: King Darius liked this idea so well that he made it a law and once it became a law, there was no way to change it. Now all of this was a trap to catch Daniel because the presidents, the governors, the princes, the counselors, and the captains were all jealous of Daniel.

AUNT SUZIE: Oh, isn't it terrible, terrible, terrible what jealousy will make a person do?

UNCLE DANDY: Yes, Aunt Suzie, it really is. That's why every boy and girl and every man and woman needs to have Jesus in their heart. Well, when it came time to pray, Daniel went to his room and he opened his window and he began to pray to God just like always. All the presidents, the governors, the princes, the counselors, and the captains were just waiting and as soon as they heard Daniel praying, they went straight to the King and told him what Daniel was doing. When the King heard it, he was so very, very, very unhappy because he loved Daniel. King Darius had made a law and it could not even be changed by him. So Daniel had to be thrown into the lions' den.

AUNT SUZIE: Oh, oh, oh, oh, oh, poor Daniel, poor Daniel, poor Daniel. Oh me, oh my.

UNCLE DANDY: Just calm down, Aunt Suzie. That's not the end of the story. Yes, they did grab Daniel and they threw him into the lions' den and the lions were hungry and you could hear the lions going Grrr, Grrr, Grrr. Then they rolled a big stone over the den and left poor Daniel.

AUNT SUZIE: Oh my, I just can't stand to see it. I just can't stand to see it. How terrible, how terrible.

UNCLE DANDY: Now Aunt Suzie, you're going to have to calm down. That's not the end of the story. Daniel got up off the floor of the lions' den and he shook himself and he looked those lions right in the eyes, and you know not one of the lions could even open his mouth. Boys and girls, do you know what happened? God sent one of His angels down and closed the lions' mouths and they walked around Daniel just like they were great big pussycats.

AUNT SUZIE: Well, praise the Lord.

UNCLE DANDY: Why yes, Aunt Suzie, it was certainly the Lord. The next morning the King came down to the lions' den real early and he said in a very weak voice, "Daniel, are you there?" And Daniel said in a strong voice, "O King Darius live forever. My God has been with me and He sent His angel to shut the lions' mouths and they have not hurt me." My, the King was so happy and he had Daniel taken up out of the lions' den. Then, Aunt Suzie, do you know what the King did?

AUNT SUZIE: He clapped his hands and he jumped for joy.

UNCLE DANDY: No, I'm afraid it was more than that. He had his soldiers throw the presidents, the governors, the princes, the counselors, and the captains into the lions' den. And the Bible says that the lions ate them all up.

AUNT SUZIE: Well, Uncle Dandy, I think this story ought to be a lesson to all of us to always do the right thing and love and serve God.

UNCLE DANDY: Yes, Aunt Suzie, that is true. Boys and girls, I hope that each of you will always try to be a Daniel.

AUNT SUZIE: Well, Uncle Dandy, I see that our time is gone.

UNCLE DANDY: Yes, Aunt Suzie, our time is gone, so boys and girls, be real good this coming week and Uncle Dandy and Aunt Suzie will see you again.

TOGETHER: Good-bye and God bless you real good. [*Both Puppets exit.*]

SWALLOWED BY A FISH

Scripture:	**Jonah 1-2**
Characters:	**2 Puppets, 1 boy and 1 girl**

GRUMPY HERMAN: [*Grumpy Herman comes onstage talking.*] What a day. What a day. What a day. The days are too long. Some of them are too short. It's too cold. What a day . . . What a day!

TAMMY: [*Tammy comes onstage talking.*] What in the world is all of this noise about? Just what is going on? Oh, oh, I might have known. It's you, Grumpy Herman.

GRUMPY HERMAN: Well, yes, it's me. Who did you expect it to be, Santa Claus?

TAMMY: Why, Grumpy Herman, why are you so grumpy today?

GRUMPY HERMAN: Well, why shouldn't I be? It looks like it may rain. I fell out of bed last night and I sat on my bubble gum. Now what's there to be happy about? You just tell me now. Just what is there to be happy about? Huh, huh, huh?

TAMMY: Well, for one thing, I'm here.

GRUMPY HERMAN: Big deal.

TAMMY: Well, all these boys and girls are here. Aren't you happy about that?

GRUMPY HERMAN: Oh, my goodness, my goodness, my goodness. I didn't even notice all those boys and girls. Oh my, oh my, oh my. Oh me, oh me, oh me.

TAMMY: Well, Grumpy Herman, I guess you're ashamed of yourself, aren't you?

GRUMPY HERMAN: Well, I guess so. But it still looks like it's going to rain.

TAMMY: Oh, Grumpy Herman, you're just impossible. There are so many wonderful things in our world and so many wonderful ways to serve God. Don't you want to serve God?

GRUMPY HERMAN: No!

TAMMY: What on earth do you mean, no?

GRUMPY HERMAN: Well, I don't mean exactly no. Well, what I mean is I do want to serve Him, but I don't want to if I have to go to Africa because if I have to go to Africa I would have to live in the jungle and eat snakes and spiders and snails and I just wouldn't like that.

TAMMY: Oh, that sounds horrible. I think I'm going to faint! Would you really have to eat those things in Africa?

GRUMPY HERMAN: Well, I'm not exactly sure, but you might have to.

TAMMY: But, Grumpy Herman, we should always do what God wants us to do. Did you know that there's a story in the Bible about a man who didn't want to go where God wanted him to go and he got into a lot of trouble.

GRUMPY HERMAN: He did! What kind of trouble?

TAMMY: Well, just let me tell you about it. And boys and girls, I want you to listen real close, too. The title of the story is "Swallowed By a Fish."

GRUMPY HERMAN: Is that really in the Bible?

TAMMY: Yes, it really is. Our story begins with God speaking to a man by the name of Jonah. God wanted Mr. Jonah to go down to the city of Nineveh and preach to the people there.

GRUMPY HERMAN: Huh. Why did He want him to go to Nineveh?

TAMMY: Well, Nineveh was a wicked city and God was going to destroy it if the people didn't turn to Him and start being good people.

GRUMPY HERMAN: Well, that was certainly a good reason to go and preach to them. Well, did Mr. Jonah go?

TAMMY: Well, no, he didn't. Jonah tried to run away from God. Jonah went down to Joppa and bought him a boat ticket and caught a boat that was going down to a place called Tarshish, and after he got on the boat he went down to the bottom of the boat trying to hide from God.

GRUMPY HERMAN: Boy! Mr. Jonah kept going down and down. In fact, I would say that he was so far down that he would have to climb a five-foot ladder to look a snake in the eye.

TAMMY: Well, I don't know about that. But he was pretty low and all because he didn't want to do what God wanted him to do.

GRUMPY HERMAN: That sounds pretty neat, though, taking a boat ride.

TAMMY:	Dear me, dear me. Oh my, my, my, my. Mr. Jonah's boat ride wasn't a very good one. In fact, it was just terrible.
GRUMPY HERMAN:	Well, Tammy, what happened? Huh, huh? Tell us. What happened, what happened? Did the boat sink? Did a giant octopus get him? Did he forget to take along some candy bars?
TAMMY:	Oh, Grumpy Herman, don't be silly. Something worse than that happened. A big storm came up and the waves were coming up over the boat and everyone in the boat was scared except Mr. Jonah and he was asleep.
GRUMPY HERMAN:	How could he sleep in a storm? I can't even sleep in my bed at home during a bad storm.
TAMMY:	Well, I don't know, Grumpy Herman, how he could sleep, but things really got bad. The storm got worse and somebody went down and woke Jonah up. And they said to him, "Get up and help us pray, for the storm is terrible." But Jonah knew why there was a storm. It was because he was disobeying God.
GRUMPY HERMAN:	Wow! What happened next?
TAMMY:	Well, Jonah said to the Captain of the ship and to all of the men, "It's all my fault. I'm running away from God and this storm is just all my fault." Then the men said to Jonah, "Well, what should we do?" And Jonah answered them and said, "If you'll throw me out into the water, the storm will stop."
GRUMPY HERMAN:	Now, I feel sick. Did, did, did they really throw him out into the water?
TAMMY:	Yes, I'm afraid they did.
GRUMPY HERMAN:	Poor Mr. Jonah. Drowned. What a way to go.
TAMMY:	Wait a minute, Grumpy Herman. Mr. Jonah didn't drown. Something else terrible happened to him.
GRUMPY HERMAN:	Oh, mercy, oh me, oh my. What could have happened to poor Mr. Jonah?
TAMMY:	Well, the Bible says that a great big fish came along and swallowed Jonah whole.
GRUMPY HERMAN:	Now *I* feel like I'm going to faint. Poor Mr. Jonah. If he had only done what God asked him to. What a terrible way to die!

Being swallowed by a fish.

TAMMY: Oh, but Mr. Jonah didn't die. He stayed three days and three nights in the fish's tummy.

GRUMPY HERMAN: Oh, Tammy. That must have been dreadful to stay three whole days and nights in the tummy of a fish.

TAMMY: Yes, it must have been. But Jonah prayed and God heard his prayer and he caused the fish to swim up to the shore, and with one big spit he spit Jonah right out on dry land.

GRUMPY HERMAN: Man! I'll bet Mr. Jonah hit the ground running toward the city of Nineveh to preach to all those bad people down there.

TAMMY: Well, I do know that Mr. Jonah did go down to Nineveh and preach because the Bible says so.

GRUMPY HERMAN: Hey Tammy. Do you think that a big fish might swallow me for not wanting to follow the Lord?

TAMMY: Well, I just don't know, Grumpy Herman. But I do know that the Lord wants you to serve Him and love Him all the time and not be so grumpy.

GRUMPY HERMAN: Oh dear me. Oh dear me. I am sorry, and I am going to do better and if the Lord wants me to go to Africa and eat snails, and snakes and spiders, I'll try it.

TAMMY: Well, Grumpy Herman. The Lord will help you. And boys and girls, the Lord will help you, too. No matter what He calls you to do, He will help you do it.

GRUMPY HERMAN: Boys and girls, Tammy's right. And you know, I don't even think it's going to rain now . . . .

TOGETHER: Bye-bye . . . . [*Both Puppets exit.*]

SHEPHERDS VISIT THE BABY JESUS

Scripture:	**Luke 2:8-20**
Characters:	**3 Puppets, 1 boy and 2 girls**

ANNABELLE: [*Annabelle and Gertrude come onstage talking.*] This is a wonderful time of the year, don't you think, Gertrude?

GERTRUDE: Oh yes, oh yes, oh yes. I do, Annabelle. I always like Christmas time. It's just so exciting!

ANNABELLE: Wow! Wow! Wow! I'll say it's exciting. Just think about all the Christmas presents.

GERTRUDE: Yes, I can just hardly wait. It's just so exciting!

WAYNE: [*Wayne comes onstage unnoticed.*] What's so exciting girls?

GERTRUDE: [*Jumps with fright.*] Oh dear me. You scared me almost to death. What do you mean sneaking up on poor innocent people like this and scaring the wits out of them?

WAYNE: Well, Miss Smarty. First of all I didn't sneak up and secondly you don't happen to be people. You are a puppet.

ANNABELLE: Don't you two like each other?

GERTRUDE: Oh yes, I guess I do. He is my big brother.

WAYNE: Oh yes indeed, Annabelle. I like my scary little sister. What are you two girls talking about?

GERTRUDE: We were talking about how excited we are about Christmas.

ANNABELLE: Wayne, don't you think Christmas is an exciting time with all the presents and things like that?

WAYNE: Yes, I sure do think that Christmas is an exciting time but not just because of Christmas presents.

ANNABELLE: Well, what else then is exciting about Christmas?

GERTRUDE: Oh, I know the answer to that. We get to visit our relatives and they get to visit us.

WAYNE: Yes, that's true, too, but Christmas means even more than just visits.

ANNABELLE:	Oh dear me, Wayne. I think I understand what you mean now.
GERTRUDE:	Well, I'm not certain that I do. Just what do you mean?
WAYNE:	Shame, shame, shame on you, Gertrude. Christmas is the celebration of Jesus' birthday.
GERTRUDE:	Oh wow! How could I have forgotten that.
WAYNE:	Well, I don't know, Gertrude. But a lot of people seem to forget that Christmas is Jesus' birthday.
ANNABELLE:	Yes, you are right, Wayne. Many, many people forget Jesus' birthday and that is sad. Wayne, would you tell us a story about Christmas.
WAYNE:	Annabelle, what kind of story do you mean?
ANNABELLE:	I mean a Bible story about Jesus being born. You know— something like that.
GERTRUDE:	Oh yes, please do, Wayne. You're the best Bible storyteller anywhere around even if you are my big brother.
WAYNE:	Well, I'm not that big but I do like to tell Bible stories.
ANNABELLE:	What story are you going to tell us, Wayne? Is it about when Jesus was born in a stable?
WAYNE:	Well girls, how would you like to hear the story, "Shepherds Visit The Baby Jesus"?
GERTRUDE:	Wow! That would be great.
ANNABELLE:	Wow! Wow! Wow! That would really be great.
GERTRUDE:	Wayne, who are shepherds? What do they do? Where do they live?
ANNABELLE:	How did they know the Baby Jesus was born? Who told them? How did they know where to find Him?
WAYNE:	Slow down, girls. Wait a minute, wait a minute.
ANNABELLE:	What's wrong with him, Gertrude?
GERTRUDE:	I don't know. That's just the way big brothers are.
WAYNE:	All right you two. Let's quit being funny. Do you really want

to hear this story?

GERTRUDE: Yep. I sure do.

ANNABELLE: Me, too.

WAYNE: All right then. You'll just have to be patient and let me start from the beginning.

GERTRUDE: Man, that would be a real good place to start. From the beginning. Don't you think that would be a good place to start, Annabelle?

ANNABELLE: Indeed I do, Gertrude. Yes, indeed I do.

WAYNE: All right you two, quit clowning around. I think I will begin with the shepherds' visit from the angel. Maybe this will answer both of your questions.

GERTRUDE: I wish you would start by telling us who the shepherds are.

ANNABELLE: Oh, I know who shepherds are. They are men who keep sheep and lead them around all day long and carry big sticks. Isn't that right, Wayne?

WAYNE: Well, Annabelle, I guess that you're right for the most part. Shepherds are men who watch after their flocks of sheep and they do carry a staff which is a large stick.

GERTRUDE: O.K. I understand who the shepherds are now. Please, now tell us about their visit to the Baby Jesus.

WAYNE: All right, let me begin with the angel's visit to the shepherds because this is really where it started.

ANNABELLE: You mean a real angel from Heaven, Wayne?

WAYNE: Yes, that's exactly what I mean, Annabelle. The night that Jesus was born in Bethlehem there were shepherds on the hillsides looking after their sheep. And suddenly an angel from Heaven came down where they were.

ANNABELLE: Oh dear me, oh dear me, oh dear me. Were the shepherds afraid?

WAYNE: Yes, Annabelle, the Bible says that the shepherds were afraid.

GERTRUDE: Well, what did the angel do?

WAYNE: The angel told the shepherds that they should not be afraid.

ANNABELLE: Wayne, the angel came to tell the shepherds about the Baby Jesus, didn't he?

WAYNE: That's right, Annabelle. The angel told the shepherds that the Baby Jesus had been born in Bethlehem, and that if they would go into Bethlehem they would find the Baby Jesus lying in a manger.

GERTRUDE: Well, what in the world happened next? Did the shepherds jump up and run to Bethlehem to see the Baby Jesus?

WAYNE: No, not at first, because after the angel told the shepherds where to find Jesus a lot of angels came down from Heaven and joined the angel and they began to praise God.

ANNABELLE: Oh, boy! That was neat.

WAYNE: Yes, it sure was, Annabelle. How wonderful it was for the shepherds!

GERTRUDE: Did all of those angels stay very long with the shepherds?

WAYNE: No, they didn't stay very long, Gertrude, and as soon as they left the shepherds ran down to the little town of Bethlehem.

ANNABELLE: Man, oh man! I think they must have been excited. I know I would have been.

GERTRUDE: Boy! I'll say.

WAYNE: Yes, they sure were excited. But they became even more excited when they saw Jesus lying in the manger.

ANNABELLE: Did they see Mary and Joseph, too?

WAYNE: Oh, yes. Yes, they saw Mary and Joseph.

GERTRUDE: Well, after they visited Jesus and Mary and Joseph what did they do?

WAYNE: Well, they went out and began to tell everyone they saw about what the angel had said, and about what they had seen.

ANNABELLE: Oh, my, my, my. Wasn't that wonderful that God sent angels down to tell shepherd men who watch after sheep, that Jesus was born.

WAYNE:	Yes, Annabelle, that was wonderful. God is a wonderful God and He wants everyone to know about Jesus.
GERTRUDE:	Now I see it. The best thing about Christmas is the birth of Jesus.
ANNABELLE:	God gave to all the world the first Christmas present, the Baby Jesus.
WAYNE:	That's right girls. That is really the true meaning of Christmas.
GERTRUDE:	Oh dear me. I'm never going to forget—ever, ever, ever again—that the most important thing about Christmas is that it's the birthday of Jesus.
ANNABELLE:	Wow! I'll say.
WAYNE:	Well, girls, I'm glad that this wonderful Bible story, "Shepherds Visit The Baby Jesus" has helped you to see what Christmas is all about.
GERTRUDE:	It sure has helped me, big brother.
ANNABELLE:	And me, too.
WAYNE:	Well, that's great girls. Well, I guess I had better be going.
GERTRUDE:	Yeah, me too. I want to get home and see what you got me for Christmas. You did get me something for Christmas didn't you, Wayne?
ANNABELLE:	Yes, that reminds me, I better get home, too, and see what I have for Christmas.
WAYNE:	Before we go girls, let's wish everyone here a very wonderful and blessed Christmas.
ALL TOGETHER:	Merry Christmas everyone! [*All Puppets exit.*]

WISE MEN VISIT JESUS

Scripture:	**Matthew 2:1-18**
Characters:	**3 Puppets, 1 boy and 2 girls**

BETTY: [*Betty comes onstage looking around.*] I told you that we were early. Annabelle, you just won't listen to me.

ANNABELLE: [*Annabelle comes onstage.*] Well, we're always late. It's not going to hurt us to be early once. Last week we were late because of your shortcuts.

BETTY: Don't you ever forget anything, Annabelle?

ANNABELLE: Not when it's about you.

BETTY: Annabelle, you're a naughty little sister.

ANNABELLE: I am not little!

FREDDIE: [*Freddie comes onstage.*] Well, hello there girls. My, you're early today. What brings you out so early?

BETTY: Annabelle just insisted on coming early so here we are.

FREDDIE: Did you girls have a good Christmas?

ANNABELLE: Oh yes. It was just the best ever.

BETTY: We sure did. Did you have a good Christmas, Freddie?

FREDDIE: I sure did. I had a very blessed Christmas. Christmas is the best time of the year when we celebrate Jesus' birthday.

BETTY: How right you are, Freddie. I'm glad that we can celebrate Jesus' birthday.

ANNABELLE: The reason Jesus came into the world as a little baby was because God loved us so much, wasn't it, Freddie.

FREDDIE: You sure are smart, Annabelle, for such a little girl.

ANNABELLE: I am not little!

BETTY: Freddie, we're ready to hear about the Wise Men that came to see Jesus after He was born.

ANNABELLE: Yeah, me too. I've been thinking all week about that.

FREDDIE:	Well, it sure is an interesting story and I would just be delighted to tell you all about it.
BETTY:	Is this story found in the Gospel of Luke, Freddie?
FREDDIE:	No, Betty, the story of the Wise Men is found in the Gospel of Matthew.
ANNABELLE:	Oh yes, I know about Matthew. Matthew is the first Gospel in the New Testament. Matthew, Mark, Luke, John, Acts ...
BETTY:	O.K. Annabelle, that's enough. I want to hear the story. I don't want to hear you. I can hear you anytime.
ANNABELLE:	Oh dear, you're going to hurt my feelings, Betty. I may even cry.
BETTY:	If you don't get quiet I'm going to hurt more than your feelings, and you will really have something to cry about.
ANNABELLE:	Well, since you put it that way, I'll get quiet.
BETTY:	I'm glad to hear that, Annabelle. Freddie, I think we're ready for the story now.
FREDDIE:	The Bible tells us that after Jesus was born Wise Men from the East came to see Him.
ANNABELLE:	Freddie, were there three Wise Men?
FREDDIE:	Annabelle, we really don't know how many Wise Men there were because the Bible doesn't tell us.
BETTY:	If the Bible doesn't tell us, then why do we hear people say that there were three?
ANNABELLE:	Yeah, Freddie, that's a good question.
FREDDIE:	Well, I think the reason people say there were three Wise Men is because there were three gifts.
BETTY:	Oh yes, now I see, Freddie.
ANNABELLE:	Yes, me too, I think!
FREDDIE:	Well, on with the story. These Wise Men were from the East and one night they saw a bright star, and they began to follow the star so that they might come and worship the Lord Jesus.

ANNABELLE:	Did they come straight to Bethlehem where Jesus was in the manger?
FREDDIE:	No, they didn't go straight to Bethlehem, Annabelle. They first went to Jerusalem.
ANNABELLE:	But why did they go to Jerusalem instead of Bethlehem?
BETTY:	Yes, I'd like to know why they went to Jerusalem and not to Bethlehem, too.
FREDDIE:	They went to Jerusalem because they thought that Jesus was there. Jerusalem was the Holy City where all the Jewish Kings lived.
ANNABELLE:	Was Jesus a Jew, Freddie?
FREDDIE:	He sure was.
BETTY:	What happened when the Wise Men got to Jerusalem? Did they start looking for Jesus?
FREDDIE:	The Wise Men went to see King Herod and they wanted to know where Jesus was so they could worship Him.
BETTY:	What did King Herod do?
FREDDIE:	The Bible says that King Herod got all of the priests and scribes together and wanted to know if they knew anything about this King of the Jews and where He would be born.
ANNABELLE:	Did they know where Jesus was going to be born?
FREDDIE:	They sure did, Annabelle. They told the Wise Men that Jesus was going to be born in Bethlehem.
BETTY:	How did they know, Freddie?
FREDDIE:	Betty, the Old Testament prophets predicted that Jesus was going to be born in Bethlehem a long, long time before He was.
BETTY:	After the Wise Men found out where Jesus was going to be born, did they go?
FREDDIE:	Yes, they did go to Bethlehem after they had a little talk with Herod.
BETTY:	You mean the King was interested in knowing where Jesus was going to be born?

ANNABELLE:	Did he want to go and worship Jesus, too, Freddie?
FREDDIE:	Well, that's what he told the Wise Men, but he really didn't want to go worship Jesus. Herod was a wicked King. He wanted to kill Him.
ANNABELLE:	Oh how terrible!
BETTY:	That sure was terrible. He must have been a wicked, wicked King.
FREDDIE:	Yes, Herod was a very wicked King.
BETTY:	Well, what happened to the Wise Men?
FREDDIE:	They followed the star right to Bethlehem.
ANNABELLE:	Freddie, you never did answer my question. Did the Wise Men come to see Jesus the night He was born?
FREDDIE:	I'm getting to that right now, Annabelle.
ANNABELLE:	That's good.
FREDDIE:	The Bible says that the Wise Men followed the star until it stopped right over the house where Jesus was living.
BETTY:	I thought Jesus was born in a stable.
ANNABELLE:	Yeah, me too.
FREDDIE:	Well, He was but you see when the Wise Men came to see Jesus it was some time since He had been born and Mary and Joseph were living in a house now.
BETTY:	Oh, now I see. The Wise Men didn't come to see Jesus the night He was born.
ANNABELLE:	Yeah, I see too. I think!
BETTY:	Well, what happened next?
FREDDIE:	The Wise Men were real happy because they had found the place where Jesus was living.
ANNABELLE:	Wow! This is a neat story. Did the Wise Men give Jesus His presents then?
FREDDIE:	They sure did, Annabelle. They gave Jesus gold, frankincense and myrrh.

BETTY:	Wow! That was great. What did they do next?
ANNABELLE:	Did they go back to Jerusalem and tell King Herod that they had found Jesus?
FREDDIE:	The Bible tells us that God spoke to the Wise Men in a dream and told them not to see Herod but to go another way.
BETTY:	Was Herod going to do something mean?
FREDDIE:	He sure was, Betty.
BETTY:	What happened next?
FREDDIE:	The Angel of the Lord came to Joseph in a dream and told Joseph to take Mary and Baby Jesus and go to Egypt so that Herod would not kill Him.
ANNABELLE:	Did King Herod get mad when the Wise Men didn't come back?
FREDDIE:	He sure did, Annabelle. He got terribly upset.
BETTY:	What did he do?
FREDDIE:	He did a terrible thing.
BETTY:	What was the terrible thing?
FREDDIE:	He had all the little boy babies in Bethlehem from two years and under killed.
BETTY:	Oh dear, oh dear. How horrible! He murdered them!
ANNABELLE:	Oh, he was a terrible man. He was a murderer; a mean murderer.
FREDDIE:	Oh yes, indeed. He was a terrible mean man. He was one of the meanest men in all the world.
BETTY:	But Jesus escaped didn't He, Freddie?
ANNABELLE:	That was because God was looking after Him, wasn't it, Freddie?
FREDDIE:	Yes, Jesus did escape because God, His Father, was looking after Him.
BETTY:	It is just so wonderful the way God looks after us.

FREDDIE: It sure is, Betty. God really loves us.

ANNABELLE: Freddie, that was a neat story.

BETTY: It sure was, Freddie. Now I know the whole story about Jesus' birth and the visit of the Wise Men.

FREDDIE: Well, I'm sure glad that you girls liked the story and I'm glad that you came today.

BETTY: We're glad that we came too. But now we'd better be going.

FREDDIE: Well, I'll see you girls next year.

ANNABELLE: Next year? That'll be a long time.

BETTY: Oh, Annabelle, next year will be next week.

ANNABELLE: Wow! Next week.

BETTY: I hope you have a Happy New Year, Freddie.

FREDDIE: I hope you and Annabelle have a Happy New Year too, Betty.

BETTY: Come on, Annabelle, it's time to go. See you next year, Freddie. [*Betty exits.*]

ANNABELLE: Wow! Wow! Wow! Next week will be next year. That sure is hard to understand. Hey, wait for me, Betty. Happy New Year, Freddie. [*Annabelle exits.*]

FREDDIE: Wow! It is hard to believe. One whole year is gone. Well, I guess I'd better go and get ready for the New Year. [*Freddie exits.*]

THE LOVE OF GOD

Scripture:	**John 3:1-17**
Characters:	**3 Puppets, 1 boy and 2 girls**

BETTY: [*Betty and Tammy come onstage talking.*] Isn't it wonderful, Tammy, how God loves us!

TAMMY: Yes, Betty, it really is. God loves all of us. Red and yellow, black and white. They're just all very precious in His sight.

GRUMPY HERMAN: [*Talking offstage.*] Oh dear, oh dear, oh dear me. How terrible, how terrible. Things are getting worse. In fact things are worse.

BETTY: What in the world is that noise?

TAMMY: I don't know but it sure sounds terrible.

GRUMPY HERMAN: [*Comes onstage talking.*] What a day, what a day, what a day. I just know it's going to be a bad day.

TAMMY: Oh me, oh me. It's you, Grumpy Herman. I might have known that it was you.

BETTY: Grumpy Herman, you're just impossible. Just why are you so grumpy?

GRUMPY HERMAN: Well, just why shouldn't I be grumpy? Just why shouldn't I be sad? Just why? Just why, just why? I want you to give me just one just why.

BETTY: Nothing could be that bad, Grumpy Herman. You're not sick. You have plenty to eat.

GRUMPY HERMAN: Well, that may be true. You noticed that I said *may* be true.

TAMMY: Being grumpy all of the time is not going to help you, Grumpy Herman. It just makes you sad.

GRUMPY HERMAN: Well, you'd be sad and grumpy too if nobody loved you.

BETTY: You don't think anybody loves you, Grumpy Herman?

GRUMPY HERMAN: I don't think anybody loves me? What do you mean I don't think anybody loves me? I mean that no, no, no, no, nobody loves me. That's what I mean. No, no, nobody.

TAMMY:	Wow! I do mean wow. That's a lot of no's.
BETTY:	Oh, be serious, Tammy.
GRUMPY HERMAN:	You see what I mean.
BETTY:	Oh, Grumpy Herman, you're just being ridiculous. Of course somebody loves you.
GRUMPY HERMAN:	Well, you just tell me one somebody who loves me. I just double-dare you to tell me.
BETTY:	That's easy. I love you, Grumpy Herman.
TAMMY:	I love you too, Grumpy Herman.
GRUMPY HERMAN:	You do? Is there anyone else?
BETTY:	There sure is, Grumpy Herman. God loves you.
TAMMY:	Yes, Grumpy Herman, God does love you.
GRUMPY HERMAN:	Oh dear. You mean God really loves one as grumpy as I am?
BETTY:	That's right, Grumpy Herman. God does love you.
GRUMPY HERMAN:	How do you know, Betty, that God loves me?
TAMMY:	Betty, why don't you tell Grumpy Herman that neat Bible story that our Sunday School teacher told us last week.
BETTY:	Oh, you mean the Bible story "The Love of God"?
TAMMY:	Yes, that's the one.
GRUMPY HERMAN:	Is this a true story? Or one that your Sunday School teacher just made up?
BETTY:	Oh dear me, oh dear me, no, Grumpy Herman. Our Sunday School teacher didn't make this story up. This story came right out of the Bible, God's Holy Word.
TAMMY:	That's right, Grumpy Herman. The best stories in all the world are Bible stories.
GRUMPY HERMAN:	Well, I guess that I want to hear this story "The Love of God" if you're sure it's a true story.
BETTY:	Oh, I'm sure that it's a true story.

TAMMY:	I'm sure it's a true story, too, because it is found in the third chapter of the Gospel of John.
GRUMPY HERMAN:	O.K. Go ahead and tell me this story. I don't think it will help much though.
BETTY:	Our story begins one night when a man by the name of Nicodemus came to see Jesus.
GRUMPY HERMAN:	Why did he come at night? Was he scared to come in the daytime?
BETTY:	I really don't know, Grumpy Herman, if he was scared to come in the daytime or not but he might have been.
TAMMY:	Yes, I think he might have been afraid to come in the daytime because Nicodemus was a religious leader and the religious leaders didn't like Jesus.
GRUMPY HERMAN:	You mean the religious leaders didn't love Jesus?
BETTY:	That's right. They didn't love Jesus. In fact, a lot of them hated Jesus.
TAMMY:	They were grumpy old men. In fact they were as grumpy as you, Grumpy Herman.
GRUMPY HERMAN:	Oh dear me, oh dear, dear me. I don't think I'm going to like this story.
BETTY:	Shame on you, Tammy. You shouldn't say things like that to Grumpy Herman.
TAMMY:	Oh, I was just teasing, Betty. I really love you, Grumpy Herman.
GRUMPY HERMAN:	I'm beginning to wonder. Betty, what did Mr. Nicodemus want?
BETTY:	Nicodemus was wanting to know all about Jesus.
GRUMPY HERMAN:	Well, what did Jesus tell him?
BETTY:	Well, Jesus began to tell Nicodemus that what he needed for his life was to become a Christian.
TAMMY:	Yes, that's true. Jesus began to tell Nicodemus that God loved him and cared for him.
GRUMPY HERMAN:	Wow! Wow! Wow! That's great. Just what did Jesus say to

him?

BETTY: Jesus told Nicodemus that God loved the world so much that He was willing to give His only Son so that Nicodemus and anyone who would could be saved.

GRUMPY HERMAN: It's true then, Betty. God does love me. Yes, it is true. God does love me.

TAMMY: Yes, it is true, Grumpy Herman. Not only does God love you but God wants to save every boy and girl and every man and woman from all their sins.

GRUMPY HERMAN: Wow! How does this happen?

BETTY: In John 3:16 we read that God loved all the people in the world so much that He let Jesus die on the cross for their sins and any who would believe in Jesus as their Saviour, God would give them a home in Heaven.

TAMMY: Oh, Betty, that is beautiful. What do you think of that, Grumpy Herman?

GRUMPY HERMAN: Wow! Wow! A triple wow! I'm just about to cry. That is beautiful.

BETTY: Yes, Grumpy Herman, this is all true and all beautiful.

GRUMPY HERMAN: God really does love everyone. Even someone grumpy like me. There's no need to be grumpy is there, Betty?

BETTY: No, Grumpy Herman, there is no need to be grumpy. Not if we believe in Jesus and accept Him as our Saviour.

GRUMPY HERMAN: You know something, Betty. I don't think I'm going to be grumpy anymore.

TAMMY: What do you mean—you don't think?

GRUMPY HERMAN: What I mean is—I know that I'm not going to be grumpy anymore. Girls, do you think that I could talk to these boys and girls for just a minute.

BETTY: I think that would be just great, Grumpy Herman. Don't you Tammy.

TAMMY: I think that would just be neat-o.

GRUMPY HERMAN: Oh thank you, girls. You're so kind. Boys and girls, I just want to tell you that God really, really does love you and that if you're not a Christian, He wants you to be. And don't ever, ever forget that wonderful, wonderful verse, John 3:16. God loved all the people in the world so much that He let Jesus die on the cross for their sins and any who would believe in Jesus as their Saviour, God would give them a home in Heaven.

BETTY: Oh dear me, that is wonderful, Grumpy Herman. Boys and girls, everything that Grumpy Herman said is true.

TAMMY: Hey, Grumpy Herman, have you ever thought about being a preacher?

GRUMPY HERMAN: Why, uh, I mean, I think . . . Oh dear me. What I'm trying to say is . . .

BETTY: Shame on you, Tammy. You're embarrassing poor old Grumpy Herman.

GRUMPY HERMAN: Man, I'll say!

TAMMY: Sorry, Grumpy Herman. I was just kidding. Betty, we can't call Grumpy Herman, Grumpy Herman anymore because he's not grumpy anymore.

BETTY: Wow! Wow! That is true.

GRUMPY HERMAN: Man, I'll say!

TAMMY: Well, let's call Grumpy Herman, Happy Herman.

BETTY: I think that's a good idea — Happy Herman. I like that.

GRUMPY HERMAN: Happy Herman. That's me. I am now Happy Herman because I know that God loves me and that you love me.

BETTY: I am just so happy for you, Happy Herman, and God does love you.

TAMMY: He sure does and so do we. Betty, let's show Happy Herman how much we love him. [*Tammy and Betty give Happy Herman a big kiss.*]

HAPPY HERMAN: Wow! Wow! Wow! Wow! Wow! Wow! Hoorah, hoorah, hoorah. Man, I'll say I'm happy! Girls, I've got to be going.

BETTY: Where are you going, Happy Herman?

HAPPY HERMAN: I'm going out to be happy. I've got a lot of catching up to do. See you later girls. [*Herman exits.*]

TAMMY: Boy! Betty, your story really helped him.

BETTY: Wow! I'll say. Boys and girls, God loves you and can make you happy if you will just let Him.

TAMMY: Let's go Betty, and be happy, too, just like Happy Herman.

BETTY: That's a neat idea, Tammy. Let's go. [*Both Puppets exit.*]

WHAT HAPPENS WHEN YOU DIE?

Scripture:	**Luke 16:19-31; Acts 7:54-60; I Thessalonians 4:13-18; John 14:1-3**
Characters:	**4 Puppets, 2 girls and 2 boys**

SAMMY: [*Sammy and Tammy come onstage talking.*] Tammy, you're just going to have to quit crying.

TAMMY: Well, I can't help it, Sammy. Poor old Harry, poor old Harry. I'm going to miss poor old Harry.

SAMMY: Well, Tammy, there's just nothing you can do about it. Things like that just happen. He's gone.

TAMMY: Oh, don't say that. Boo, hoo, hoo, hoo, boo, hoo, hoo, hoo, oh boo, hoo, hoo, hoo.

SAMMY: Wow! This is worse than a rainstorm. Tammy, if you don't quit I'm going to have to get my umbrella.

TAMMY: Oh, you're just mean. Mean, mean, mean, Sammy. Boo, hoo, hoo, hoo. Oh boo, hoo, hoo, hoo.

FREDDIE: [*Freddie and Betty come onstage talking.*] What's going on here?

BETTY: Dear me, dear me. What's going on, what's going on, what's going on? Why are you crying, Tammy?

TAMMY: Oh boo, hoo, hoo, hoo. Oh boo, hoo, hoo, boo, hoo, hoo.

SAMMY: Oh, Tammy's crying because Harry, her goldfish, died.

FREDDIE: Tammy, those kinds of things happen every day. You'll just have to learn to live without Harry.

BETTY: That's right, Tammy. My pet bird, Tweety-Pie, died last year. You know everything has to die sometime.

SAMMY: Yes, that's what I've already told her but she won't listen to me.

TAMMY: You mean everything? You mean my cat, Freckles?

FREDDIE: Yes, Tammy, I'm afraid so. Even people die.

TAMMY: Oh dear, oh dear. It's even worse than I thought.

BETTY:	I have a good idea. Freddie, you seem to know a lot about the subject of dying. Would you tell us what happens when a person dies?
SAMMY:	Wow! That would be a good idea.
TAMMY:	Yes, I guess that might be a good idea.
FREDDIE:	Gee whiz, I don't know much about this subject. But I'll try to tell you what the Bible says.
BETTY:	Wow! That'll be neat, Freddie.
SAMMY:	It sure will because the Bible has the answer to everything.
TAMMY:	Freddie, where does a person go when he dies?
FREDDIE:	In the sixteenth chapter of Luke, you know that's one of the Gospels, Jesus told the story about a rich man who died and a poor man who died. The rich man was not a good man, and when he died Jesus said he went to a place called Hell.
BETTY:	Oh yes, I've heard about that place. That's a terrible place where people go who are not Christians.
SAMMY:	Yes, I've heard about that awful place, too.
TAMMY:	Oh dear me, yes, I've heard about that dreadful place. There's a lot of fire in Hell isn't there, Freddie?
FREDDIE:	I'm afraid you're right, Tammy. The Bible does tell us that Hell is a place where there is fire. And this is the kind of place that the rich, mean man went to.
SAMMY:	Christians won't ever go to Hell, will they, Freddie?
FREDDIE:	Oh no, Sammy. All Christians have been saved from their sins and they'll never go to Hell.
TAMMY:	What happened to the poor, good man who died?
FREDDIE:	Well, Jesus said that the poor good man went to Heaven.
TAMMY:	Heaven's a wonderful place isn't it, Freddie?
FREDDIE:	It sure is, Tammy.
BETTY:	Every Christian that dies goes to Heaven to be with Jesus and live with Him forever and ever.

SAMMY:	Yes, that's right, Betty. The Bible teaches us that.
FREDDIE:	Yes, that's certainly true. Every Christian that dies goes to Heaven and Heaven is a wonderful place.
BETTY:	Freddie, I remember reading in the Bible about a man named Stephen who went to Heaven. Do you remember that story?
FREDDIE:	Oh yes, I remember that story. It's found in the Book of Acts.
SAMMY:	Some mean men killed Mr. Stephen, didn't they?
FREDDIE:	Yes, that's right. Stephen was a deacon and he was teaching all about Jesus and some of the people didn't like that. They got so mad that they took Stephen outside the city and they began to throw rocks at him.
TAMMY:	You mean they were trying to kill him with rocks?
FREDDIE:	That's right, Tammy. And while these big rocks were hitting him in the head and stomach, Stephen looked up into Heaven and he saw Jesus standing in Heaven, and in just a minute a great big rock hit Stephen and he died. Then he went to Heaven.
TAMMY:	Poor, poor Stephen.
SAMMY:	Well, Tammy, it was bad the way they killed Stephen. But he got to go to Heaven and that was wonderful.
BETTY:	Yes, that's true but when someone dies don't they bury their body in the ground?
FREDDIE:	Yes, Betty, they do.
BETTY:	You mean, their body doesn't ever go to Heaven?
FREDDIE:	Oh no, Betty. Someday every Christian that dies will have his body again.
SAMMY:	How can this happen?
TAMMY:	Wow! This sounds spooky.
FREDDIE:	Oh, there's nothing spooky about this. The Bible tells us that someday Jesus will call every Christian's body to come out of the ground and to come to Heaven.
BETTY:	Will our bodies be just like they are now?

FREDDIE:	Not just exactly, Betty. God is going to make our bodies all new. They'll never get old again. They'll never be sick. Oh, it's all going to be just wonderful.
TAMMY:	You're right, Freddie, that is wonderful. It's not spooky.
BETTY:	Man! That is great!
SAMMY:	Yes, it really is. Dying is really not bad after all, is it?
FREDDIE:	Sammy, the Bible says that it's a good thing when the Christian dies because he goes to live with Jesus forever and ever.
TAMMY:	Freddie, are you sure that there's going to be enough room for every Christian in Heaven?
BETTY:	Yes, that's a good question, Tammy. I know a lot of Christians.
FREDDIE:	Girls, you won't have to worry about that. There is plenty of room in Heaven. The Bible tells us this.
SAMMY:	Do you have a scripture in the Bible that tells us about this?
BETTY:	Yes, I would like to know if there's a scripture passage that tells us this wonderful thing of there being enough room in Heaven for all the Christians.
TAMMY:	Wow! Wow! I'd like to know a scripture passage like that. I would make it my memory verse.
FREDDIE:	Yes, I do have a Bible passage for you. In the Gospel of John, the fourteenth chapter, verses 1-3, Jesus tells us that He has gone to Heaven to build a home for all Christians. And all the Christians would one day live with Him in that home.
BETTY:	Is that the scripture where Jesus talks about mansions?
TAMMY:	What's a mansion?
SAMMY:	That's a great big old house that people live in.
TAMMY:	You mean we're going to live in a great big house in Heaven?
FREDDIE:	Oh, no, no, Tammy. We're not going to live in a great big house. What Jesus meant was that Heaven was going to be a big place, and there would be room enough for every Christian to live there and every Christian would have a

place.

SAMMY: Wow! That is neat.

BETTY: I'll say! That really is neat!

TAMMY: I really feel better now.

FREDDIE: I sure am glad, Tammy, that you're feeling better.

SAMMY: You know, I'm not afraid to die now because I know what happens.

BETTY: Thank you, Freddie, for helping us to understand what happens when you die.

SAMMY: Well, I'd better go. I've got to go home and feed my frog.

TAMMY: Oh dear, oh dear, oh me, oh dear. Did you say a frog? One of those green, slimy things? I think I'm going to faint. Oh, I think I'm going to faint.

SAMMY: Here we go again. Come on, Tammy, we don't have time for you to faint now. [*Sammy and Tammy exit.*]

FREDDIE: We'd better go too, Betty. I've just got to feed me.

BETTY: Oh, you boys. All you ever think of is eating. [*Both Puppets exit.*]

THE GOOD SAMARITAN

Scripture:	**Luke 10:30-37**
Characters:	**2 Puppets, 2 girls**

BETTY: [*Comes onstage talking to herself.*] I just don't have time. I've got too many other things that I've got to be doing. I just don't have time; that's all there is to it.

TAMMY: [*Comes up behind Betty.*] Just what do you mean, Betty, you don't have time?

BETTY: [*Jumps and hollers.*] Wow! Tammy, you sure did scare me!

TAMMY: I'm sorry, Betty. I didn't mean to scare you. What is your problem?

BETTY: Oh, it's that Mrs. Jones, our Sunday School teacher. She's always talking to us about helping someone and calling them our neighbors. But my neighbors don't need any help.

TAMMY: Oh dear, dear, dear, dear me. Betty, you shouldn't feel like that.

BETTY: And just why, may I ask, shouldn't I feel like that?

TAMMY: Well, it's just not right, that's why.

BETTY: And who says it's not right?

TAMMY: Well, the Bible says it's not right.

BETTY: Does the Bible say that I should help people that are not my neighbors?

TAMMY: Why yes, Betty. The Bible does say that. That's the reason Mrs. Jones, our Sunday School teacher, is wanting us to help other people in our town, not just those who live next door, for the Bible tells us that we should never be too busy to help other people.

BETTY: Well, I guess that you and Mrs. Jones are right, but I always thought that my neighbors were those people who live right around my house.

TAMMY: You're not the only one who has thought that.

BETTY: I'm not?

TAMMY:	No, you're certainly not, Betty. Jesus tells us in the Bible about a lawyer who wanted to know who his neighbor was.
BETTY:	Wow! A lawyer is an important person, and smart. What did Jesus tell him?
TAMMY:	Well, Jesus told him a story about a good Samaritan who helped a stranger.
BETTY:	Tammy, would you tell me the story about "The Good Samaritan"?
TAMMY:	Why yes, Betty. I would be delighted to do that. In fact, I would be greatly delighted to do that.
BETTY:	I'm ready.
TAMMY:	Jesus said that a certain man was traveling from Jerusalem to a place called Jericho.
BETTY:	Oh yes, I've heard of Jericho. That's where the walls fell down. Oh dear me. I've interrupted you, Tammy. Please go on.
TAMMY:	Well, on his way from Jerusalem to Jericho, some robbers jumped out from behind a rock and they grabbed the poor man and they beat him up . . . .
BETTY:	Oh dear, oh dear. How horrible! How terrible! That was even bad.
TAMMY:	Why, I should say it was. After they beat him up, they robbed the poor man. They took all of his clothes and all of his money and they left him on the road half dead.
BETTY:	Oh, that poor man. Did someone come along and help him?
TAMMY:	Well, it wasn't long until a priest came down the road.
BETTY:	Oh goodie, goodie, goodie. Help was on the way.
TAMMY:	Well, Betty, I'm sorry to say that the priest wouldn't help him.
BETTY:	You mean he wouldn't stop? A priest?
TAMMY:	I'm afraid he wouldn't. In fact he walked by on the other side of the road. He wouldn't even go by and look at him. The priest didn't think that the man was his neighbor and that he needed to help him.

BETTY: Oh dear, oh dear. But he needed help. Did someone else come and help him?

TAMMY: Well, next a Levite came down the road.

BETTY: Oh yes, I know about the Levites. They were very religious men. I know he helped him.

TAMMY: No, Betty. I'm afraid not. Jesus says that he just came over and looked at the man, then went back over to the other side of the road and went walking down it as fast as he could.

BETTY: Oh, oh, oh. How terribly, terribly, terribly dreadful. That poor, poor man didn't have one single neighbor.

TAMMY: Oh, yes he did. There came down the road a Samaritan, and as soon as he saw the poor hurt man, he jumped down off from his donkey and ran over to him as fast as he could.

BETTY: Oh, goodie, goodie, goodie. What did he do next?

TAMMY: Well, he began to wash him and put bandages on his wounds, and then he helped him onto his donkey.

BETTY: Oh, how wonderful and exciting this is. What did he do next? Where did he take him?

TAMMY: Well, he took him to the nearest Inn.

BETTY: What in the world is an Inn, Tammy? Is that a hospital?

TAMMY: Oh no, Betty, that was like a hotel or motel like we have today. It was a place where travelers would stay.

BETTY: Oh yes, now I remember Mrs. Jones, our Sunday School teacher, telling us a story of Mary and Joseph and how there was no room for them in the inn. Well, what did this good Samaritan do after he got the poor man to the inn?

TAMMY: Well, he put him in a bed and gave the innkeeper some money to look after this man until he was well again and could travel.

BETTY: Oh, what a wonderful story! The good Samaritan really was a neighbor, wasn't he?

TAMMY: Yes, Betty, he was, and Jesus was pleased with the good Samaritan.

BETTY: Oh, oh, oh. Dear me. Oh me, oh my. I am so ashamed of the way I've been acting. Tammy, I want to be a neighbor to everyone, no matter where they live.

TAMMY: Oh, I'm just so glad Betty. Because Jesus wants each of us to be a good Samaritan and to help our neighbors all over the world.

BETTY: Oh, yes, yes, yes. I can see that now. I'm going to go out and help others just like the good Samaritan did.

TAMMY: That's just wonderful, Betty. And boys and girls, don't you forget to be a good Samaritan to everyone, everywhere. Betty, would you like to hear another story?

BETTY: Oh, dear me, no Tammy. We don't have time. We've got to go out and be a good Samaritan. Hurry! We don't want to be late! [*Both Puppets exit.*]

THE BOY WHO DIDN'T WANT TO STAY AT HOME

Scripture:	**Luke 15:11-24**
Characters:	**2 Puppets, 1 boy and 1 girl (both young)**

TOGETHER: [*Betty and Freddie come onstage together.*] Good morning, boys and girls.

BETTY: Isn't it just wonderful to be back in the House of the Lord, and especially to be at Children's Worship?

FREDDIE: Indeed, indeed, indeed it is. It's just so good to see all of you boys and girls. Is everybody happy?

BETTY: My, Freddie. I believe that everyone here this morning is happy.

FREDDIE: Why, I do declare, Betty. I believe, yes, I do believe you're right.

BETTY: Freddie, when we serve the Lord and do what is right, this makes us happy, doesn't it?

FREDDIE: Why, yes indeed, Betty, it does. Boys and girls, if you love the Lord Jesus and let Him come into your heart and life, obey your mother and father and your teachers, and do what is right and good, you will be happy.

BETTY: Oh, Freddie. I know that this is just true. But why are so many people not happy today?

FREDDIE: Well, Betty, I'm glad you asked that question.

BETTY: Oh, me. Here comes a story.

FREDDIE: Betty!

BETTY: Sorry.

FREDDIE: Betty, the reason many people, and even boys and girls are not happy, is because they don't want to let the Lord Jesus have their life. And this does remind me of a story.

BETTY: Is it a story about someone who was not happy?

FREDDIE: Yes, Betty, it is. In fact, it's the story about "The Boy Who

Didn't Want To Stay At Home."

BETTY: Freddie, is this a Bible story?

FREDDIE: Why yes, indeed, Betty. It really is. This is the story right out of God's Book — the Bible.

BETTY: Well, what in the world happened?

FREDDIE: Well, the story begins in a home where there were two boys, and one of these boys was happy and one of these boys was not happy.

BETTY: Oh, dear me, oh dear me, oh dear me. Why was one of them not happy? Was his father mean to him?

FREDDIE: Oh gracious me, no! He had the kindest father in all the world.

BETTY: Well then, why on earth was he unhappy?

FREDDIE: Well, he didn't want to stay at home. He wanted to do everything his way. So one day he said to his father, "Father, I'm going to leave. Give me all that belongs to me. I'm just not happy here at home."

BETTY: Well, dear me, dear me, dear me. What happened? Did he leave?

FREDDIE: Well, yes, he did, Betty. He packed his clothes. And he took all of his money, put it in his pocket and left.

BETTY: Well, then was he happy?

FREDDIE: Well, he thought so. This is just what he wanted—he thought.

BETTY: I bet his father wasn't happy. And why do you keep saying he thought he was happy?

FREDDIE: Well, that's a good question, Betty. Sometimes people think they're happy with what they're doing, but they find that their happiness turns to sadness.

BETTY: Is this what happened to this young man? Did his happiness turn to sadness?

FREDDIE: Yes it did.

BETTY: What happened? Dear me, what happened?

83

FREDDIE: Betty, if you will keep quiet so I can finish the story, you'll find out.

BETTY: Remember, Freddie. Be happy.

FREDDIE: Betty, you're just impossible. Well, this young man traveled a long way from home, and he met a lot of new friends and he started spending his money and having wild parties. He was really living it up.

BETTY: Sounds like he was pretty happy to me.

FREDDIE: Well, Betty, it wasn't long until he ran out of money, and when he ran out of money he ran out of friends and he found himself all alone.

BETTY: Oh, dear me. Did he not have just one friend left?

FREDDIE: Oh, dear me, no Betty. Not even one friend. And he was hungry and he had no place to sleep, and my how unhappy he was again.

BETTY: Oh dear, oh dear, oh dear. How sad, how sad. Oh my, oh me. What in the world did he do?

FREDDIE: Betty, things got so bad that he went out to a hog farm and the farmer gave him a job feeding the hogs. And he was so hungry that he would almost eat the hogs' food.

BETTY: Oh dear, oh dear. How sad, how sad. That poor dear boy. Nobody loved him.

FREDDIE: Oh, yes, there was someone that loved him, Betty.

BETTY: Who?

FREDDIE: His father still loved him. And he was waiting for him back home.

BETTY: Did he go back home to his father?

FREDDIE: Well, not at first, but one day when he was hungry and lonely and so, so, sad he said to himself, "Why the servants in my father's house have more to eat, to wear, and are happier than I am. I think I'll go home and say to my father . . ."

BETTY: Oh dear me, oh dear me, oh dear me. I just can't wait, I just can't wait. What did he say? What did he say to his father?

FREDDIE:	Just calm down, Betty, and I'll tell you. He said to himself, "I'll tell father that if he'll just let me come back home, I'll be one of his servants."
BETTY:	Well, did he?
FREDDIE:	Well, Betty. He didn't get a chance to.
BETTY:	Oh dear, oh dear. Did robbers or somebody do something mean to him before he got home? Did, did, did he die?
FREDDIE:	Oh, no, Betty. Nothing like that happened. His father one day was looking down the road and he saw his son way down the road. And his father ran out to meet him.
BETTY:	Oh dear, then what happened?
FREDDIE:	His father put his arms around him and he said, "Son, I love you and I'm glad you're back home." And then he called to his servants and had them bring a robe and put it on his son, and they put a ring on his finger and new shoes on his feet.
BETTY:	Oh dear, oh dear. How exciting, how exciting!
FREDDIE:	Oh, yes it was. The very next thing he did, he told one of his servants to go kill the best and the fattest calf because they were going to have a big party because his son was back home.
BETTY:	You mean his father didn't fuss at him for wasting all of his money and losing all of his clothes?
FREDDIE:	Oh dear me, no. His father forgave him and loved him.
BETTY:	I'll bet that young man was really, really, happy this time, wasn't he?
FREDDIE:	Oh, yes, yes, yes, yes, yes. He really was happy. Because now he was doing the right thing.
BETTY:	Freddie, I'm glad that I'm happy.
FREDDIE:	Yes, Betty, I'm glad that you are, too. And boys and girls, I hope that all of you are happy because you are serving Jesus and doing what's right.
BETTY:	Boys and girls, never, ever, never be like the boy who didn't want to stay at home.

FREDDIE: That's right, boys and girls. Don't ever, ever be. Well Betty, we better be going.

TOGETHER: Boys and girls, don't forget to have a happy day today and every day. [*Both Puppets exit.*]

THE PARABLE OF THE TEN VIRGINS

Scripture:	**Matthew 25:1-13**
Characters:	**2 Puppets, 1 man and 1 woman (both elderly)**

AUNT SUZIE: [*Aunt Suzie and Uncle Dandy come onstage together talking.*] Uncle Dandy, isn't it so wonderful to know that Jesus is coming again?

UNCLE DANDY: Why, Aunt Suzie, indeed it is. It is indeed. It is just so wonderful, wonderful, wonderful.

AUNT SUZIE: Uncle Dandy, look who is here.

UNCLE DANDY: Wow! Wow! If it isn't all of the nice boys and girls that we've been missing. Hello boys and girls. It's just so good to see you again.

AUNT SUZIE: My, oh my, oh me. It is so good to see all of you boys and girls. And it's just so good to be back with you here at Children's Worship.

UNCLE DANDY: Boys and girls, Aunt Suzie and myself were just talking about a very important thing that is going to happen someday.

AUNT SUZIE: Why yes, boys and girls, we were talking about Jesus and one day He's going to come back for all Christians.

UNCLE DANDY: I get so excited thinking about Jesus coming again.

AUNT SUZIE: Yes indeed, yes indeed, yes indeed. This is just so exciting.

UNCLE DANDY: Boys and girls, did you know that Jesus was coming again someday? It's just going to be so wonderful.

AUNT SUZIE: Uncle Dandy, do you have a dandy story that you might tell the boys and girls about Jesus and His coming again?

UNCLE DANDY: Why, Aunt Suzie, I just thought you'd never ask. Yes, I do have a story and as always it's right out of the Bible.

AUNT SUZIE: Boys and girls, all of the best stories come out of the Bible, God's Holy Word.

UNCLE DANDY: Yes indeedy, deed, deed, deed they do.

AUNT SUZIE: Well, what is the title of the story?

UNCLE DANDY:	The title of the story is "The Parable Of The Ten Virgins."
AUNT SUZIE:	Gracious me, gracious me, Uncle Dandy. What in the world is a parable?
UNCLE DANDY:	Now that's a good question, Aunt Suzie. And some of the boys and girls at Children's Worship know the answer to that question.
AUNT SUZIE:	Yes, I guess they do. But some of us don't know so I think you had better tell us.
UNCLE DANDY:	O.K. I'll just do it. Here we go. A parable is an earthly story with a heavenly meaning.
AUNT SUZIE:	Uncle Dandy, you sure are smart.
UNCLE DANDY:	Well, now that you mentioned it, I guess I might be. But let's see how many of the boys and girls know the answer. Boys and girls if you know the answer, put your hand up real high.
AUNT SUZIE:	My, my, my. You certainly were right, Uncle Dandy. Now how about telling us this earthly story with a heavenly meaning.
UNCLE DANDY:	O.K. Here we go.
AUNT SUZIE:	You mean we're ready now?
UNCLE DANDY:	Yes, Aunt Suzie, if you'll quit interrupting me. This parable is found in the Gospel of Matthew. And it's about ten young women who were waiting for a wedding party to start.
AUNT SUZIE:	Oh my, that's exciting.
UNCLE DANDY:	Yes, Aunt Suzie, it is exciting. Where Jesus lived they did things a lot different than the way we do them now. These ten young women were waiting, watching and listening for the man that was getting married to come. And they had to be ready because he could come at anytime. And if they were not ready to go in with him when he went into the house and closed the door, they would miss the wedding party.
AUNT SUZIE:	Well mercy me, my, my. What if they got tired and sleepy and fell asleep?
UNCLE DANDY:	Well, Aunt Suzie, that's just exactly what happened to these ten young women. They set their lamps down and while they were talking and waiting they just fell asleep.

AUNT SUZIE: Well, what in the world happened next? And what were the lamps for?

UNCLE DANDY: My, my, gracious me. Aunt Suzie, I just declare. It was dark.

AUNT SUZIE: Well, why didn't you say so?

UNCLE DANDY: Well, I just did. O.K. Back to the story.

AUNT SUZIE: Yes, yes, yes. Let's get back to the story. Did those poor girls miss the wedding party because they were asleep?

UNCLE DANDY: Oh, I do declare, Aunt Suzie, if you wouldn't interrupt me I could go on with the story.

AUNT SUZIE: Oh dear me. I'm sorry, Uncle Dandy. But I'm just so excited. Please go on.

UNCLE DANDY: Well, while these ten young women were asleep someone shouted, "The bridegroom is coming." And all ten of these young women jumped up and they grabbed their lamps and they began to fill them with oil for the wedding party. And then a terrible thing happened.

AUNT SUZIE: Oh dear me, oh dear me. Did one of them drop the lamp?

UNCLE DANDY: No, Aunt Suzie, it was worse than that. Five of these young women did not have any more oil.

AUNT SUZIE: Oh dear, oh dear. What did they do, borrow from the other five?

UNCLE DANDY: Well, they tried to but there just wasn't enough. They had to have their own oil for the wedding party, so they rushed off to try to buy some.

AUNT SUZIE: Oh dear, what happened next?

UNCLE DANDY: Well, while they were gone to try to find some more oil, all the people who were coming to the wedding and the five young women who had oil all went in for the wedding party and they closed the door.

AUNT SUZIE: Oh, those poor girls. Those poor girls. What happened to those five girls?

UNCLE DANDY: Well, they found some oil somewhere and they came rushing back and they knocked on the door but it was just too late. The wedding party had already started and they couldn't get in.

AUNT SUZIE:	Oh, Uncle Dandy, how terrible, terrible, terrible.
UNCLE DANDY:	Yes, Aunt Suzie, it is terrible. But did you know that this is what's going to happen to all of those who are not Christians when Jesus comes back?
AUNT SUZIE:	Oh, yes, Uncle Dandy. The Bible tells us that we must be watching and waiting and that means all of us, doesn't it?
UNCLE DANDY:	Yes, Aunt Suzie, it does. And boys and girls, if you're not a Christian and Jesus comes back before you become a Christian, you would be like the five young women. You would be left out. But boys and girls, Jesus loves you and me and He died on the cross to take away our sins.
AUNT SUZIE:	Yes, boys and girls. In John 3:16 Jesus says, "For God so loved the world, that he gave his only begotten Son, that whosoever believeth in him should not perish, but have everlasting life."
UNCLE DANDY:	So boys and girls if you're here today and you haven't asked Jesus to come into your heart, won't you do it today so when Jesus comes, He can take you with Him.
AUNT SUZIE:	Oh, Uncle Dandy. I'm just so excited about Jesus coming again.
UNCLE DANDY:	Yes, Aunt Suzie, we should be. But we should never forget that we should be waiting, watching and working. Well, boys and girls, it looks like Aunt Suzie and Uncle Dandy had better be going for today. Remember to . . .
TOGETHER:	Keep looking up, for Jesus is coming. It may be morning. It may be noon. It may be evening. It may be soon. Good-bye and God bless. [*Both Puppets exit.*]

THE LAST SUPPER

Scripture: **Mark 14:12-26**
Characters: **4 Puppets, 2 boys and 2 girls**

UNCLE CHARLIE: [*Comes onstage talking.*] I wonder where those kids are [*looks out at audience*]. Dear me, what a wonderful group here today. My name is Uncle Charlie. I am supposed to meet my nephew and nieces here today. I promised to tell them a Bible story and since you're here I'll let you listen in, too. I wonder where those kids are.

WAYNE: [*Talking offstage.*] You two have made us late. It's all your fault. Yes, yes it's all your fault.

UNCLE CHARLIE: Well, well, well, now I know where those kids are.

GERTRUDE: [*All three come onstage together.*] It is not my fault. It is positively not my fault.

WAYNE: Well, whose fault is it then?

GERTRUDE: It's all Susie's fault. We would not have been late if it had not been for Susie.

SUSIE: Everything that happens in this family is my fault, and it's all because I'm the littlest sister.

WAYNE: You mean smallest don't you?

SUSIE: You stay out of this, biggest brother.

UNCLE CHARLIE: Hold on, hold on, hold on. What's going on here? What's all the commotion about?

GERTRUDE: What commotion, Uncle Charlie?

SUSIE: Yeah, what commotion, Uncle Charlie?

WAYNE: Did you hear any commotion, Uncle Charlie?

UNCLE CHARLIE: Yes, I'm afraid I did and I'm not going to ask you why you're late because I think that's what the commotion's all about.

WAYNE: Uncle Charlie, those two sisters of mine are always late and they cause me to be late. I mean they're always late.

SUSIE: I am not always late.

GERTRUDE:	Yes, you are. It's all your fault. If you hadn't gotten locked in the closet we would have been on time.
SUSIE:	Well, it was your fault, Gertrude. You closed the door.
WAYNE:	You see what I mean, Uncle Charlie.
UNCLE CHARLIE:	Indeed, I do. I do, indeed. I think I indeed do, or is it I do indeed see?
GERTRUDE:	Well, we're here, Uncle Charlie, and we're ready for a Bible story.
SUSIE:	Yes, we want to hear a Bible story from God's Holy Word.
WAYNE:	That's right, Uncle Charlie. My favorite stories are Bible stories.
UNCLE CHARLIE:	Well, I'm glad that you kids like Bible stories because they are the best stories in all the world.
WAYNE:	Wow! Wow! Wow! Wow! Wow! Look out there. Who are they?
UNCLE CHARLIE:	Who is who?
WAYNE:	Wow! Wow! Wow! Wow! Wow! I mean who are all these people, especially the girls?
GERTRUDE:	Well, what about the boys?
SUSIE:	Yes, what about that cute little boy? You see him, the one with the big grin on his face?
UNCLE CHARLIE:	Oh, you mean all of these boys and girls? Oh, they've come to hear a Bible story just like you have. It's so good to have all of these boys and girls here today.
SUSIE:	It sure is, especially that littlest boy with the big grin.
WAYNE:	Susie, you mean the smallest boy.
SUSIE:	He may be smallest to you but he's littlest like me.
GERTRUDE:	O.K. you two, pipe down. Uncle Charlie wants to tell us a Bible story don't you, Uncle Charlie?
UNCLE CHARLIE:	Yes, Gertrude, I think that I'm ready if you are, to tell you one of my favorite Bible stories.
WAYNE:	What's the title of your Bible story, Uncle Charlie?

UNCLE CHARLIE: Well, I thought that I would tell you the story entitled "The Last Supper."

GERTRUDE: Where is this story in the Bible, Uncle Charlie? Is it found in the Gospels?

SUSIE: Is it a true story, huh? Is it a true story? Is it, is it, is it? I mean is it really a true story?

UNCLE CHARLIE: One question at a time girls.

WAYNE: Yeah, Uncle Charlie, that's the way they do to me when I tell them a Bible story.

UNCLE CHARLIE: Our story is found in the Gospel of Mark in the fourteenth chapter, and it most certainly is a true story. I do mean a true, true story.

WAYNE: Uncle Charlie, is it the story about the time that Jesus was in the upper room with His disciples?

GERTRUDE: Oh yes, yes, yes, yes. I know something about that. It's when Jesus broke bread.

SUSIE: How can you break bread? All mine ever does is crumble.

GERTRUDE: Oh, Susie, you don't know anything do you?

SUSIE: Yes, Miss Smarty, I do know something. I know about the time that you . . .

GERTRUDE: That will be enough of that, Susie.

WAYNE: You two get quiet so Uncle Charlie can get on with the story.

UNCLE CHARLIE: That's a good idea, Wayne. Let's get on with the story. Our story takes place the day before Jesus was crucified on the cross.

WAYNE: Oh yes, this is the story that I know about. This is the story of the Lord's Supper, isn't it?

UNCLE CHARLIE: Yes, Wayne, at this Last Supper Jesus did leave for all of us the wonderful part of our church service that we call the Lord's Supper.

SUSIE: Oh I think I understand now, Uncle Charlie. Please tell us this exciting story.

UNCLE CHARLIE: Well, our story begins with Jesus telling two of His disciples

	to go into the city of Jerusalem, and there they would see a man carrying a pitcher of water.
GERTRUDE:	What were they supposed to do when they saw this man carrying a pitcher of water?
UNCLE CHARLIE:	Jesus told His two disciples to follow the man.
SUSIE:	Was the man going to give Jesus' disciples some water to drink?
WAYNE:	Oh dear me no, little sister.
SUSIE:	It's littlest, biggest brother.
UNCLE CHARLIE:	No, Susie, the disciples didn't want a drink of water. Jesus told His disciples to follow the man to his house. And when they arrived at his house they were to ask which room was prepared for Jesus and His disciples to eat their supper in.
GERTRUDE:	Did the disciples find the man and the house just like Jesus said they would?
UNCLE CHARLIE:	Yes, everything was just like Jesus said it would be.
SUSIE:	Jesus knows everything doesn't He, Uncle Charlie?
UNCLE CHARLIE:	Yes. He sure does, Susie.
WAYNE:	Did Jesus and all His disciples go to the house for supper that night?
GERTRUDE:	That's called the Upper Room, isn't it, Uncle Charlie?
UNCLE CHARLIE:	That's right, Gertrude. The house had an upper room.
SUSIE:	What's an upper room?
UNCLE CHARLIE:	Well, that's what we would call today an upstairs room, Susie.
SUSIE:	Oh, I see. Well, what happened next?
UNCLE CHARLIE:	Well, what happened next is a very wonderful story. In fact, it's a beautiful story.
WAYNE:	Oh, I remember what happened now, Uncle Charlie. This is where Jesus began the Lord's Supper that we have in our churches.

UNCLE CHARLIE: That's right, Wayne. While they were eating Jesus took some

bread and He asked God to bless it; then He broke it and He gave some to all of His disciples and said for them to eat it.

GERTRUDE: Why did Jesus do this?

UNCLE CHARLIE: Well, He was trying to help His disciples see that He was going to die on the cross.

WAYNE: Jesus also told them to drink some wine, didn't He?

UNCLE CHARLIE: Yes, after Jesus blessed the bread and broke it and gave to His disciples to eat He also blessed the cup of wine and then told them to drink some of it. You see the bread was supposed to be His body and the wine His blood.

SUSIE: Was the bread really Jesus' body and the wine really Jesus' blood?

UNCLE CHARLIE: Oh dear, no, no, no, Susie. This was only to remind Jesus' disciples and all Christians today why Jesus died and how He died.

WAYNE: Uncle Charlie, this is the reason then that Christians have the Lord's Supper in church.

UNCLE CHARLIE: Yes, that's right, Wayne. All Christians are to remember how much Jesus loves them.

SUSIE: Does Jesus love just Christians?

GERTRUDE: Oh no, Susie. Jesus loves everybody. That's the reason He died on the cross.

UNCLE CHARLIE: Yes, that's true. Jesus does love everybody and that's the reason He died on the cross.

WAYNE: But the Lord's Supper is just for Christians isn't it, Uncle Charlie?

UNCLE CHARLIE: That's right, Wayne. When we come to church and have the Lord's Supper that's just for Christians.

GERTRUDE: Now, I understand, Uncle Charlie, why you called this story "The Last Supper." It was the last supper that Jesus ate with His disciples before He was crucified on the cross. Isn't that right?

UNCLE CHARLIE: That's right, Gertrude. This was the last supper that Jesus ate with His disciples before He was crucified on the cross.

WAYNE: Would you tell us about Jesus being crucified, Uncle Charlie?

GERTRUDE: Yes, would you please, Uncle Charlie, would you please?

UNCLE CHARLIE: Well, I would be just delighted to but first of all there is a story that ought to come next before Jesus' crucifixion on the cross.

SUSIE: What story is that, Uncle Charlie?

UNCLE CHARLIE: It's the sad story of the trial of Jesus.

GERTRUDE: You mean Jesus was tried, like in a court?

UNCLE CHARLIE: Yes, that's what I mean.

GERTRUDE: Oh dear, oh dear, oh dear. How terrible, how terrible, how terrible.

WAYNE: Would you tell us that story now, Uncle Charlie?

UNCLE CHARLIE: Oh dear me no. Our time is gone for today. But if you would come back next week I would tell you the story right out of the Bible of "The Trial Of Jesus."

WAYNE: Oh, we'll be back.

GERTRUDE: And we'll be on time if we can keep Susie out of the closet.

SUSIE: You're just picking on me because I'm the littlest sister.

WAYNE: You mean smallest. [*Susie, Gertrude and Wayne exit.*]

SUSIE: [*Talking offstage.*] I mean, I mean, I mean littlest, littlest, littlest, biggest brother.

UNCLE CHARLIE: Well, I sure hope they'll be on time next week. And boys and girls, you be sure and be back for another exciting Bible story right out of the Bible, God's Holy Word. See you next week. [*Uncle Charlie exits.*]

THE TRIAL OF JESUS

Scripture:	**Mark 14:53 — 15:19; Matthew 26:57 — 27:26**
Characters:	**4 Puppets, 2 boys and 2 girls**

GERTRUDE: [*Wayne, Gertrude, and Susie come onstage talking.*] Where is Uncle Charlie? I don't see him anywhere around.

SUSIE: You mean we're early. You mean we're early. I just can't believe that we're early. I only got to wash one ear this morning and I only got to comb half of my hair and now we're early.

WAYNE: Well, what's wrong with being early?

GERTRUDE: There's nothing wrong with being early. But being this early is ridiculous.

SUSIE: Well, I'm sure glad it's not my fault. Because most of the time I get blamed and it's all because I'm the littlest sister.

WAYNE: You mean the smallest.

UNCLE CHARLIE: [*Comes onstage talking.*] Well, I see that you are on time today.

GERTRUDE: I'll say on time. We've been here for a long time. Our clock at home must be fast.

SUSIE: Wow! I'll say; real fast.

GERTRUDE: You can say that again, Susie.

SUSIE: Wow! I'll say; real fast.

GERTRUDE: Will you stop that, Susie!

SUSIE: Oh, you're picking on me again.

UNCLE CHARLIE: Wayne, are your sisters always like this?

WAYNE: Oh no, not always. Just while they're awake.

GERTRUDE: You're going to get it, big brother.

SUSIE: Yeah, you're going to get it, biggest brother.

UNCLE CHARLIE: If you girls will calm down, I think we're ready for another

Bible story. You girls ought to be ashamed of yourselves. All those boys and girls are out there waiting for a Bible story and here you are arguing.

WAYNE: Oh, those two are ashamed, Uncle Charlie.

GERTRUDE: You're going to get it. Whoops, I'm sorry.

SUSIE: Yes, I think I'm sorry too.

UNCLE CHARLIE: All right now. That's better.

WAYNE: Uncle Charlie, we're ready for the Bible story.

SUSIE: Yes, we're ready.

UNCLE CHARLIE: I believe that all of these boys and girls here are ready for the Bible story too.

GERTRUDE: Then it looks like we're all ready for you to tell us the Bible story "The Trial Of Jesus."

UNCLE CHARLIE: Our Bible story begins today with Jesus and His disciples coming down from the Upper Room after the Last Supper.

WAYNE: Jesus went into the garden to pray, didn't He, Uncle Charlie?

UNCLE CHARLIE: Yes, that's exactly what Jesus did, Wayne. He took His disciples and went into a garden to pray. After Jesus had prayed some men came and took Him away.

GERTRUDE: Oh, I remember all about that. One of Jesus' own disciples brought those wicked men, didn't he?

UNCLE CHARLIE: Yes, that's true, Gertrude. It was Judas who brought these men to arrest Jesus.

SUSIE: You mean one of His own disciples did this to Jesus?

UNCLE CHARLIE: Yes, Susie, Judas betrayed Jesus to the wicked men.

SUSIE: Boy! Judas was a wicked men too, wasn't he.

WAYNE: You mean wicked man, don't you?

SUSIE: Men or man, he was still mean.

UNCLE CHARLIE: Yes, Judas was a very mean man to do something as bad as that.

GERTRUDE: Well, what did these men do when Judas brought them to arrest Jesus? Did they beat Him up and drag Him away?

UNCLE CHARLIE: No, they didn't beat Him up but they did arrest Him.

GERTRUDE: What did Jesus' disciples do? Did they try to help Him escape?

WAYNE: Peter pulled out his sword and whacked off one man's ear.

GERTRUDE: Is that really true, Uncle Charlie?

UNCLE CHARLIE: Yes. I'm afraid it is, Gertrude.

SUSIE: Hooray, hooray, hooray for Peter. I bet that made Jesus happy, didn't it?

UNCLE CHARLIE: No, Susie, that didn't make Jesus happy. He was very sad that Peter would cut off the ear of another man. Jesus touched the poor man's ear and healed it.

GERTRUDE: That just goes to show how much Jesus loves people. When people were mean to Jesus, He was good to them.

WAYNE: Uncle Charlie, tell us what happened next.

UNCLE CHARLIE: Well, the Bible tells us that they took Jesus to the home of the High Priest. All of the religious leaders were waiting for them so that they could try Jesus.

GERTRUDE: Why did these people want to try Jesus? What was He guilty of?

WAYNE: Jesus was not guilty of anything, was He, Uncle Charlie?

UNCLE CHARLIE: No, Jesus was not guilty of anything mean. The religious leaders of that day did not like Jesus because He was doing good and teaching people the truth.

GERTRUDE: Well, what happened to Jesus?

UNCLE CHARLIE: These wicked men found other wicked men who would tell lies about Jesus.

SUSIE: It's bad to tell lies.

UNCLE CHARLIE: It sure is, Susie. These wicked men told so many lies that what they said made each other a liar.

WAYNE: Well, how did they find Jesus to be guilty, then?

UNCLE CHARLIE:	They didn't find anything that Jesus was guilty of, and finally the High Priest asked Jesus if He was the Son of God.
GERTRUDE:	Jesus was the Son of God and is the Son of God and will always be the Son of God. Isn't that right, Uncle Charlie?
UNCLE CHARLIE:	That is true, Gertrude. Jesus is and was and will always be the Son of God.
WAYNE:	What did these wicked men do when Jesus answered the High Priest?
UNCLE CHARLIE:	Jesus answered the High Priest by telling him that He was the Son of God. This made the High Priest and all those around him so mad that they began to shout that Jesus should be killed.
SUSIE:	Oh dear, oh dear. How terrible, how terrible. Just for telling the truth these men wanted to kill Jesus.
UNCLE CHARLIE:	Yes, I'm afraid you're right, Susie. They did want to kill Jesus for telling the truth.
GERTRUDE:	Did these wicked religious leaders kill Jesus?
UNCLE CHARLIE:	No, they couldn't kill Jesus because it was against the law.
WAYNE:	Oh yes. I know about that. The religious leaders were Jews. But the people who made the laws in that day were Romans.
UNCLE CHARLIE:	You're pretty smart, Wayne.
GERTRUDE:	He sure is.
SUSIE:	That's because he's my biggest brother.
UNCLE CHARLIE:	Please girls. Yes, Wayne, it was the Romans who made the laws in those days and that meant that the Jews had to take Jesus to the Romans for them to try Him, too.
GERTRUDE:	You mean Jesus had to be tried twice?
UNCLE CHARLIE:	Yes, that's true, Gertrude. Jesus had to be tried twice. First by the religious leaders. Then next by the Romans.
WAYNE:	The Roman leader who tried Jesus was named Pilate, wasn't he?
UNCLE CHARLIE:	Yes, that's exactly right. His name was Pilate. The religious leaders put chains on the hands of Jesus and sent Him to

	Pilate, the Roman Governor.
SUSIE:	Oh, that was mean. Poor Jesus. All He ever did was help people and now they're being mean to Him.
UNCLE CHARLIE:	Yes, Susie, that's certainly true. They were being mean to Jesus.
GERTRUDE:	What did Governor Pilate do? Did he find Jesus guilty like the religious leaders did?
UNCLE CHARLIE:	No, Governor Pilate did not find Jesus guilty.
SUSIE:	Did he let Jesus go?
WAYNE:	Pilate was a scaredy-cat wasn't he, Uncle Charlie.
UNCLE CHARLIE:	Yes, he sure was.
GERTRUDE:	I thought you said that Pilate was the Governor. I didn't think governors were scared of anything.
SUSIE:	What was Governor Pilate scared of?
UNCLE CHARLIE:	He was scared that the religious leaders would cause a lot of trouble and maybe even cause him to get fired.
GERTRUDE:	Well, if Jesus wasn't guilty and Pilate wouldn't let Him go, what did he do?
UNCLE CHARLIE:	They had a custom in that day that at this particular time of the year, which was a special holiday for the Jews, the Roman Governor would let a criminal who was in jail go free. So on this particular day the Roman Governor decided to let the people decide whether they wanted this mean criminal to be set free or Jesus.
WAYNE:	The religious leaders got the people to shout for the Governor to let the criminal go, didn't they?
UNCLE CHARLIE:	Yes, I'm afraid that's true, Wayne.
GERTRUDE:	That's terrible. That's just terrible. That was not much of a trial.
UNCLE CHARLIE:	I'm afraid you're right, Gertrude.
SUSIE:	What happened to Jesus?
UNCLE CHARLIE:	Well, Susie, that's another story.

WAYNE: You're not going to stop now are you, Uncle Charlie? Won't you tell us the story of "Jesus Crucified"?

UNCLE CHARLIE: Wayne, I'm afraid I won't be able to tell you that story today because our time is gone again. But if you and Gertrude and Susie would come back next week, and if all of you boys and girls will come back next week, I will tell you the story "Jesus Crucified."

GERTRUDE: We sure will be back next week, Uncle Charlie. We love to hear Bible stories, even if they are sad like today's Bible story was.

UNCLE CHARLIE: Well, we will meet here next week at the same time and at the same place. See you all next week. [*All Puppets exit.*]

JESUS CRUCIFIED

Scripture:	**Matthew 27:26-66; Luke 23:33-56**
Characters:	**4 Puppets, 2 boys and 2 girls**

WAYNE: [*Comes onstage talking.*] Come on you two. What's keeping you?

GERTRUDE: [*Comes onstage talking.*] What do you mean what's keeping us? We're right behind you.

WAYNE: Well, where is Susie?

GERTRUDE: Oh Susie's like the cow's tail. She is always last.

SUSIE: [*Comes onstage talking.*] I heard that. I heard that. I am not a cow's tail. And biggest brother, my legs are not as long as yours. You walk faster than I do. I'm just the littlest sister and that's why you pick on me.

WAYNE: Don't you mean smallest, Susie?

SUSIE: No, I don't mean that. I mean littlest because I am the littlest.

UNCLE CHARLIE: [*Comes onstage talking.*] Well, kids, I can hear that you're all here.

WAYNE: Oh, Uncle Charlie, that's just Susie.

SUSIE: Uncle Charlie, they're just picking on me.

GERTRUDE: We are not, Uncle Charlie. All I said was that Susie's always last like a cow's tail.

SUSIE: See what I mean, Uncle Charlie? They're always picking on me because I am the littlest girl.

UNCLE CHARLIE: Well, well, well. Let's all get calmed down now. Look at all those boys and girls out there. They've come to hear a Bible story, not to hear you kids argue.

SUSIE: Wow! You're right, Uncle Charlie, they are out there. I'm sorry, Uncle Charlie. I'm ready for a Bible story.

GERTRUDE: Yes, me too, Uncle Charlie. I'm sorry and I'm ready for a Bible story.

103

WAYNE:	Uncle Charlie, I believe that our Bible story today is the story of Jesus being crucified, isn't it?
UNCLE CHARLIE:	Yes, Wayne, that is true. Our Bible story today is entitled "Jesus Crucified."
GERTRUDE:	Uncle Charlie, this is another true story, isn't it?
UNCLE CHARLIE:	Yes, Gertrude it is. This story is right out of the Bible, God's Holy Word.
SUSIE:	Well I'm ready for the Bible story today. Will you please begin, Uncle Charlie?
UNCLE CHARLIE:	If you will remember, last week my story ended with Governor Pilate not wanting to kill Jesus, but the religious leaders caused such a fuss and demanded that Jesus be crucified that Governor Pilate let it happen.
WAYNE:	That was a terrible thing that Governor Pilate did.
UNCLE CHARLIE:	Yes, it sure was, Wayne.
SUSIE:	Well, what happened next, Uncle Charlie? I just can't wait to hear.
UNCLE CHARLIE:	Well, the Bible says that the soldiers took Jesus and they beat Him with a whip.
GERTRUDE:	Oh dear me, oh dear me, oh dear me. That is terrible, terrible, terrible.
UNCLE CHARLIE:	Yes, Gertrude, that was terrible but that's not all they did. They took off Jesus' clothes and put a scarlet robe on Him, and then they put a crown of thorns on Jesus' head, and then they spit on Him and hit Him over the head with a stick.
GERTRUDE:	Oh dear, oh dear, oh dear. That was just terrible. Poor Jesus.
SUSIE:	Did Jesus try to hit them and punch them in the nose for being mean to Him?
WAYNE:	Oh goodness no, dear me no, Susie. Jesus didn't do a thing to them. He loved them and felt sorry for them.
UNCLE CHARLIE:	That's right, Wayne. Jesus loved them and He loves us, too.
SUSIE:	What happened next? What did they do to Jesus after they were so mean to Him?

UNCLE CHARLIE: They made Jesus pick up a big old heavy cross, and they started out of town where they were going to crucify Jesus.

WAYNE: They were going to a place called Mt. Calvary, I think. Isn't that right, Uncle Charlie?

UNCLE CHARLIE: Yes, Wayne, that's right. The soldiers led Jesus up to Mt. Calvary.

GERTRUDE: Did Jesus have to carry that heavy cross all the way up to the mountain?

UNCLE CHARLIE: Gertrude, it wasn't a big mountain. It was more like a hill that was called Mt. Calvary. No, Jesus didn't carry the cross all the way to Mt. Calvary. The Bible says that He fell and the soldiers got a man out of the crowd to carry the cross for Jesus.

SUSIE: Uncle Charlie, do you know that kind man's name?

UNCLE CHARLIE: Yes, Susie. The Bible says that his name was Simon.

GERTRUDE: Well, I'm sure glad that there was a good kind man like Simon there to carry Jesus' cross.

WAYNE: The next thing that happened was the worst thing of all, wasn't it, Uncle Charlie?

SUSIE: What could be worse than beating Jesus and spitting on Him and hitting Him over the head with a stick.

UNCLE CHARLIE: Well, the crucifixion was the worst thing that happened to Jesus.

GERTRUDE: Being crucified means that Jesus was nailed to the cross, doesn't it, Uncle Charlie?

UNCLE CHARLIE: Yes, I'm afraid it does, Gertrude. They made Jesus lie down on top of the cross and the soldiers took great big old nails and nailed Jesus' hands and feet to the cross. Then they picked it up and dropped it in a hole.

GERTRUDE: Oh dear me, dear me, dear me. That was so terrible.

SUSIE: Did Jesus still love everybody?

UNCLE CHARLIE: Yes, Susie, He did. Jesus asked God to forgive all of those men who were mean to Him and who were killing Him.

WAYNE: That would really be hard to do. I just don't know if I could do that or not.

UNCLE CHARLIE: Yes, Wayne, that would be hard to do. But if you love people like Jesus did then He will help you to love people who are mean to you.

GERTRUDE: Did Jesus die on the cross that day?

UNCLE CHARLIE: Yes, He did. The Bible tells us that Jesus did.

SUSIE: What happened next?

UNCLE CHARLIE: The Bible tells us that two kind men by the name of Joseph and Nicodemus placed Jesus' body in Joseph's very own tomb.

SUSIE: What's a tomb, Uncle Charlie?

UNCLE CHARLIE: Well, a tomb in those days, Susie, was a room or a cave in the side of a hill where they would bury people that had died.

WAYNE: Jesus didn't stay in the tomb though did He, Uncle Charlie?

UNCLE CHARLIE: No, Wayne, He sure didn't. On the third day, Jesus came back to life.

GERTRUDE: Wow! Wow! Wow! This story has a real happy ending. Jesus is still alive today, isn't He?

UNCLE CHARLIE: Yes, Gertrude, Jesus is still alive today and Jesus wants to save everyone from their sins.

SUSIE: You mean Jesus even wants to save boys and girls from their sins?

UNCLE CHARLIE: That's right, Susie. Jesus died on the cross and came back to life again so that He could save boys and girls, mothers and fathers, everybody even that wants to be saved.

WAYNE: Man, oh man! This is great.

SUSIE: This is neat.

GERTRUDE: Jesus is wonderful.

UNCLE CHARLIE: That's right, kids. Jesus is wonderful.

GERTRUDE: Uncle Charlie, this story has really helped me.

SUSIE: Me too, Uncle Charlie.

WAYNE: Uncle Charlie, these three stories, "The Last Supper," "The Trial Of Jesus," and "Jesus Crucified" are just the best.

UNCLE CHARLIE: Well, I'm so glad that you three like my stories from the Bible, and I hope that all these boys and girls have liked my Bible stories.

WAYNE: Well, little sisters. I guess we had better be going. See you soon, Uncle Charlie. [*Wayne exits.*]

GERTRUDE: Yes, I guess we'd better be going. Thank you, Uncle Charlie for all of these Bible stories. [*Gertrude exits.*]

SUSIE: You tell the neatest Bible stories, Uncle Charlie. Just the neatest.

GERTRUDE: [*Talking offstage.*] Come on little cow's tail. We're going to be late for lunch.

SUSIE: There she goes. She's picking on me again just because I'm the littlest sister. I'm coming. [*Susie exits.*]

UNCLE CHARLIE: Well, boys and girls, I'd better go too. I hope to see you again real soon. [*Uncle Charlie exits.*]

IT'S NEVER TOO LATE TO SING

Scripture:	**Acts 16**
Characters:	**2 Puppets, 1 boy and 1 girl**

SAMMY: [*Sammy comes onstage talking.*] Oh my, I just wish I didn't have to go. I just wish I didn't have to go.

TAMMY: [*Tammy comes onstage talking.*] What in the world is all of this commotion? Oh, it's you, Sammy. I might have known. What are you complaining about?

SAMMY: Oh, I don't want to go to Sunday School and Children's Worship.

TAMMY: Oh, Sammy. You know it's not nice to talk like that. You don't really mean it, do you?

SAMMY: No, I guess I don't. But it just seems so hard getting up every Sunday morning and studying and then doing all that singing at Children's Worship.

TAMMY: Oh, you just ought to be ashamed of yourself. Just what if you had to go through all the things that poor Paul and Silas did.

SAMMY: What do you mean all of the things Paul and Silas did? Who are Paul and Silas? Are they those new kids down the street?

TAMMY: No, silly, Paul and Silas are two men found in the New Testament. They were on a missionary journey. Let me tell you the story of "It's Never Too Late To Sing."

SAMMY: Hey, Tammy, who are they?

TAMMY: Oh, my goodness, Sammy. This must be Children's Worship. Hello, boys and girls. My name is Tammy and this is my brother, Sammy, and we're just so happy to be here today.

SAMMY: Yes, boys and girls, we really are. Tammy's just been helping me to see the need to come to Sunday School and Children's Worship every Sunday. Boys and girls, Tammy was just about to tell me a story, a very exciting story about Paul and Milas.

TAMMY: No, no, no, no, no, Sammy. It's not Paul and Milas. It's Paul and Silas.

SAMMY:	Well, anyway, it has something to do with late singing, or singing too late, or something like that.
TAMMY:	Oh, Sammy, I do declare. There must be something wrong with your hearing. The title of the story is "It's Never Too Late To Sing." Boys and girls, would you like to hear the story, too?
SAMMY:	Well, what are we waiting for?
TAMMY:	Not a thing. Our story begins in the city of Philippi with Paul and Silas preaching and teaching the gospel. Every day while Paul and Silas were preaching, a young woman who had an evil spirit living in her would bother them.
SAMMY:	Wow, wow, wow. That must have been creepy.
TAMMY:	Yes, Sammy, I guess it was. But one day Paul, in the name of Jesus, said to the evil spirit, "come out of this girl right now," and the evil spirit came right out.
SAMMY:	Wow, wow, wow, wow. That was neat.
TAMMY:	Yes, it was, but it got Paul and Silas in a lot of trouble.
SAMMY:	You mean some people didn't want the evil spirit to come out of the girl?
TAMMY:	That's right, Sammy. There were some evil men there that didn't want that evil spirit to come out of the girl. Well, they called the police and had Paul and Silas thrown in jail.
SAMMY:	You mean for preaching and doing good?
TAMMY:	I'm afraid so, Sammy.
SAMMY:	Boy! Am I glad that I didn't live back then.
TAMMY:	Well, that's what happened to Paul and Silas. But before they threw them in jail, they took off their clothes and beat them.
SAMMY:	Wow, wow! That must have been embarrassing, and I guess it hurt too.
TAMMY:	Oh, Sammy, you're just impossible. You know it hurt.
SAMMY:	Yes, it must have. I know when Dad gives me five lashes with the switch it really hurts.

109

TAMMY:	Most of the time you need ten. Would you quit interrupting so I can finish this story?
SAMMY:	Yes, yes. I'm sorry. Go ahead.
TAMMY:	Well, after they had beaten Paul and Silas, they put them way back in the prison and chained their feet so that they could not move around. Paul and Silas were bleeding and hungry and a long way from home. But do you know what they did?
SAMMY:	No, what did they do, do, do, do. Huh, huh!?
TAMMY:	Well, at midnight Paul and Silas began praying and singing, and all the prisoners heard them.
SAMMY:	You mean they weren't embarrassed?
TAMMY:	No, they didn't care who heard them. But best of all God heard them and He sent a great earthquake and the whole prison shook, and all the doors flew open and all the chains came loose from the prisoners.
SAMMY:	Boy! Was that place all shook up!
TAMMY:	It sure was and the jailor was so scared that he was going to kill himself, but Paul and Silas wouldn't let him.
SAMMY:	You mean they didn't hate him for beating them and putting them in prison?
TAMMY:	Oh, no. They loved the jailor and that very night they helped him to come to know Jesus as his Saviour, and all of his family.
SAMMY:	Well, what happened to Paul and Silas?
TAMMY:	Well, the next day they let Paul and Silas go.
SAMMY:	Boy, Tammy, that was a wonderful story. I'm never going to complain about going to Sunday School and Children's Worship. I want to learn more about Jesus, so that I can love people like Paul and Silas. And I'm never going to complain again about singing in Children's Worship either!
TAMMY:	Well, that's just wonderful, Sammy. I'm so glad that you want to be like Paul and Silas. Jesus loves everyone of us very, very much and He always wants us to sing praises to Him.

SAMMY: Tammy, is it too late for us to sing a song with the boys and girls?

TAMMY: Oh, my, Sammy, "It's Never Too Late To Sing."

SAMMY: Well, then let's sing, "Jesus Loves Me." Boys and girls, will you help us? [*They all sing together.*]

TAMMY: My boys and girls. That was real, real good.

SAMMY: Well, Tammy, we had better be going.

TAMMY: Yes, Sammy, we had. Good-bye boys and girls and don't forget . . .

SAMMY: "It's Never Too Late To Sing" and don't complain. Bye . . . [*Both Puppets exit.*]

A STORM AT SEA

Scripture:	**Acts 27:1-37**
Characters:	**3 Puppets, 1 boy and 2 girls**

TAMMY: *[Tammy and Gertrude come onstage talking.]* I just like exciting Bible stories from the Bible, God's Holy Word. Don't you, Gertrude?

GERTRUDE: Yes, Tammy, the best and most exciting stories in all the world are Bible stories. I wish we had someone that could tell us an exciting Bible story right now, don't you?

TAMMY: I sure do, yes, I positively do. Absolutely I do.

SAMMY: *[Sammy comes onstage talking.]* Well, what's happening, Tammy? Who's this young lady with you?

TAMMY: Hello, Sammy. This is my friend, Gertrude. Gertrude, this is my friend Sammy.

GERTRUDE: Hi, Sammy.

SAMMY: Well how do you do, do, do. It is a pleasure to meet you. It's always good to have a pretty new face around for a change.

TAMMY: Oh dear, oh dear. Oh me, oh my. You're hurting my feelings, Sammy. I may just cry.

SAMMY: Oh, Tammy, I was just teasing you.

TAMMY: You had better be just teasing me.

SAMMY: I was, Tammy. What are you girls up to?

GERTRUDE: We were just wishing, Sammy, that we had someone to tell us an exciting Bible story.

SAMMY: Well, isn't that something. I was just wishing that I had someone to tell an exciting Bible story to.

TAMMY: Sammy, I've never seen you when you didn't have an exciting Bible story to tell. We would be delighted if you would tell us an exciting, exciting Bible story.

GERTRUDE: Yes, would you? Huh, huh, huh? Would you, huh?

SAMMY: Well, how exciting of a story do you want? One that is exciting, more exciting, or super exciting?

GERTRUDE: I want to hear a super exciting Bible story don't you, Tammy?

TAMMY: Oh yes, I think I feel like a super exciting story today. What's it going to be, Sammy?

SAMMY: Well, girls, I think that I will tell you the story entitled "A Storm At Sea."

GERTRUDE: Wow! That sounds exciting.

TAMMY: I'll say!

SAMMY: If you girls are ready, I'll begin. This story is about the Apostle Paul.

TAMMY: Oh, yeah, I know about Paul. He was a great missionary.

SAMMY: That's right. Paul was a great missionary. And he loved God and obeyed God in all things.

GERTRUDE: Was Paul on one of his missionary trips when he got caught in this storm at sea?

SAMMY: Well, not exactly. You see Paul was on his way to Rome to stand trial before Caesar, the ruler of the world.

TAMMY: Oh dear me, oh dear me, oh dear me. What did Paul do that was wicked?

SAMMY: Paul didn't do anything wicked. The religious leaders did not like Paul preaching and teaching about Jesus.

GERTRUDE: Poor Paul. Well, tell us what happened to Paul on his way to Rome.

SAMMY: Well, Paul was not the only prisoner going to Rome, there were others. Paul and the other prisoners were placed on a ship and an officer of the Roman Army was placed in charge of Paul and all the other prisoners.

TAMMY: Was this a great, big ship with three smokestacks?

SAMMY: Oh dear me no, Tammy. Boats in those days didn't have smokestacks. They had sails.

TAMMY: Well, what in the world are sails?

GERTRUDE:	Oh, I know what sails are. Sails are big old sheets on a pole and when the wind blows they get big and make the ship move.
TAMMY:	Oh, you mean that Paul was on a sailboat.
SAMMY:	Well, this was not exactly a sailboat. It did have sails but it was bigger than our sailboats. And it was the wind that made the ship move.
TAMMY:	Wow! I wouldn't want to travel like that across the sea.
GERTRUDE:	Wow! I would. I think that would be an exciting way to travel. Tell us what happened, Sammy. I just can hardly wait to hear this story.
SAMMY:	Well, for the first day or two Paul had good sailing but then the wind started to blow in the wrong direction and they had difficulty in traveling. They finally stopped at a place called Fair Havens for a few days. By the time they got ready to sail to Rome the weather was getting bad.
TAMMY:	You mean it was getting dangerous, don't you, Sammy?
SAMMY:	Yes, that's exactly what I mean. This was the wrong time of the year now to sail to Rome.
GERTRUDE:	Well, did they go ahead and set sail?
SAMMY:	Yes, I'm afraid they did, Gertrude, but before they did Paul tried to talk the officer in charge of the prisoners into not going.
TAMMY:	Did Paul know that something bad was going to happen?
SAMMY:	Yes, I think he did because Paul told them that if they left Fair Havens they might have a shipwreck and maybe some people might be killed.
GERTRUDE:	They just wouldn't listen to Paul though, would they?
SAMMY:	No, they sure wouldn't. They didn't think Paul knew what he was talking about.
TAMMY:	Well, what happened next? Did they have a shipwreck?
SAMMY:	They set sail for Rome and everything went just fine. It looked like they were going to have a good day to sail. But that didn't last long.

TAMMY:	Oh dear me, oh dear me, oh dear me. What happened, what happened?
SAMMY:	The wind began to blow and it wasn't long until the ship was bobbing up and down in the ocean like a cork and they were in a terrible, terrible predicament.
GERTRUDE:	Wow! Wow! Wow! Wow! This story is really getting exciting.
TAMMY:	I'll say exciting. I think I'm going to be sick.
SAMMY:	Here we go again. Tammy, we haven't even gotten to the worst yet.
TAMMY:	Oh dear me, oh dear me. I know I'm going to be sick.
GERTRUDE:	Oh tell us more, tell us more, Sammy.
SAMMY:	Well, the next day things were worse. The waves got higher and the wind was stronger. Things were so bad that the sailors began throwing their cargo overboard.
TAMMY:	Oh dear, oh dear. Things are getting worse and I'm feeling worse.
GERTRUDE:	Tell us more Sammy, tell us more.
SAMMY:	This terrible, terrible storm kept on for many, many days until everyone on the ship had given up hope, except for Paul, of ever seeing land again.
TAMMY:	You mean Paul knew something that no one else knew?
SAMMY:	That's right, Tammy. Paul told everyone on the ship not to be afraid because an angel from God had spoken to him and said that no one would be drowned in this storm.
GERTRUDE:	You mean then that there would not be a shipwreck and they would all go to Rome safely.
SAMMY:	No, Paul didn't mean that the ship would not wreck because he told all the men that the ship would wreck, but no one would drown; everyone would be saved.
TAMMY:	How many days had this terrible storm been going on?
SAMMY:	Paul and these poor men had been in the storm for about fourteen days.

GERTRUDE:	Wow! Wow! Wow! That was a long, long time.
SAMMY:	Yes, that was a long time. About two weeks they were in that storm.
GERTRUDE:	Well, what happened next? Did the ship wreck?
SAMMY:	Around midnight on the fourteenth day they discovered that land was close by, and the next morning Paul told all the men that they had better eat something for they had not eaten for a long time.
TAMMY:	Dear me, dear me. How long had it been since these poor men had had anything to eat? Were they not hungry?
SAMMY:	Tammy, it had been about two weeks since they had had anything to eat. I guess they were just too scared and too sick to their stomachs to eat.
TAMMY:	Oh dear me. Sick to their stomachs. I think I'm going to faint.
SAMMY:	Oh, Tammy, you're acting like a little baby. Just think about poor Paul and those men. They didn't act that way.
GERTRUDE:	God was really looking after Paul, wasn't He, Sammy.
SAMMY:	Yes, Gertrude. He certainly was. God always looks after His people. God was also looking after the other 276 men on that ship.
TAMMY:	Wow! Wow! Wow! You mean there were 276 men aboard the ship during the storm?
SAMMY:	That's right, Tammy, 276.
GERTRUDE:	Wow! Wow! This is exciting. What happened next?
SAMMY:	Something terrible was about to happen. There was going to be a great shipwreck. So Paul told everyone on board to get something to eat and he also told all of them that none of them would be hurt.
TAMMY:	Oh, how wonderful it is the way God looks after His own men and women.
SAMMY:	Yes, it is, Tammy. It is so wonderful.
GERTRUDE:	Oh, how exciting, how exciting! Did the ship wreck? What happened when it wrecked?

SAMMY: I'm sorry girls but we're out of time. You'll just have to come back next week to hear my exciting story about the great shipwreck.

GERTRUDE: Oh no, no, no. Please tell us what happened.

TAMMY: No use, Gertrude. We'll just have to come back next week.

SAMMY: That's right girls. If you'll come back next week and if all you boys and girls come back next week we'll find out what happened to Paul as I tell you the story of "The Great Shipwreck."

GERTRUDE: See you next week.

TAMMY: Me, too.

SAMMY: Be looking for you all. Good-bye until next week. [*All Puppets exit.*]

THE GREAT SHIPWRECK

Scripture:	**Acts 27:38 — 28:11**
Characters:	**3 Puppets, 1 boy and 2 girls**

GERTRUDE: [*Gertrude and Tammy come onstage together.*] Come on, come on, come on, Tammy. We don't want to be late.

TAMMY: Slow down, Gertrude, we're not going to be late. I've never seen anyone more excited than you.

GERTRUDE: Wow! Wow! Wow! I am excited. I can hardly wait to hear how God rescues Paul from a shipwreck.

TAMMY: Well, Gertrude, you'll just have to wait because I don't see Sammy here anywhere. I guess we'll just have to wait for him.

GERTRUDE: Well, Tammy, we're not the only ones waiting for Sammy. Look at all those boys and girls. They're waiting too. And they sure do look excited.

SAMMY: [*Comes onstage talking.*] Who's excited?

GERTRUDE: Oh hello, Sammy, we're excited. I mean I'm excited. All these boys and girls are excited.

SAMMY: Well, what's all the excitement about?

TAMMY: Oh Sammy, you know what we're excited about. We're excited about the Bible story that you're going to tell us today, "The Great Shipwreck."

GERTRUDE: Boy! I'll say. I just could hardly wait to get back to hear this exciting story.

SAMMY: Since everyone's ready, I'll begin my story. Last week we left Paul and all the men on the ship still in the storm but close to some land.

GERTRUDE: It was nighttime wasn't it, Sammy?

SAMMY: Yes, it sure was. They couldn't see a thing. Not only was it dark but the wind was blowing, it was raining and the waves were crashing against the boat.

TAMMY: Oh dear me, oh me. How scary, how scary.

SAMMY:	Yes, Tammy, it must have been terribly scary. But finally the day came and they saw land.
GERTRUDE:	Did they know where they were?
SAMMY:	No, I'm afraid they didn't. They didn't have the slightest idea where they were. But they did see a wide opening that they hoped would take them up to the beach. So the captain of the ship started to sail his ship into that little opening.
GERTRUDE:	I thought you said this was the story of a shipwreck.
SAMMY:	That's just exactly what happened next, Gertrude. The ship ran up on a big sandbar.
TAMMY:	Dear me, dear me. What is a sandbar, Sammy?
SAMMY:	Well, a sandbar is sort of like a pile of sand out in the water and it's mostly under the water and you can't see it until it's too late.
GERTRUDE:	What happened next? Oh it's just so exciting. Please tell us what happened next.
SAMMY:	The ship got stuck on the sandbar and the big old waves began to beat against the ship and the ship started to come apart.
TAMMY:	You mean the ship was coming apart in the water?
SAMMY:	Yes, that's right. The captain of the guards told all of his prisoners to jump overboard and start swimming for the land.
TAMMY:	Oh dear me, oh dear me. Those poor men, poor old Paul. What did they do if they couldn't swim?
SAMMY:	Well, they had to grab a piece of the ship that had broken off or a log or something.
GERTRUDE:	Did everyone get to land safely?
SAMMY:	They sure did, Gertrude.
TAMMY:	Paul knew they would didn't he, Sammy?
SAMMY:	Yes, he sure did, Tammy. God had sent one of His angels to tell Paul that everyone on the ship would be saved when it wrecked.

GERTRUDE:	God always keeps His promises and always looks after His people, doesn't He, Sammy?
SAMMY:	Yes, that's one thing that we can always depend on. God will always keep His promises.
TAMMY:	Well, where did Paul land? What was the name of this land?
SAMMY:	Well, Paul and all the other men soon learned that they were on an island and the name of the island was Malta.
GERTRUDE:	Did anyone live on this island?
SAMMY:	Oh yes, there were some very friendly people that lived on the island. They built a big fire so that everyone could get warm.
GERTRUDE:	I'm sure glad that Paul was safe. Nothing could hurt him now, could it?
SAMMY:	Well, a bad thing did happen. Paul was getting sticks to put on the fire and all of a sudden a big poisonous snake reached out and bit Paul on the hand.
TAMMY:	A snake, a snake, oh dear me, a snake. I'm going to faint. Oh I know I'm going to faint. [*She faints.*]
SAMMY:	Wow! Wow! She did faint. Get up, Tammy, get up.
GERTRUDE:	Dear me, dear me. Does she faint often?
SAMMY:	Not often. Just when she hears about snakes.
TAMMY:	Oh dear, oh dear. I feel terrible. Poor Paul, poor Paul.
SAMMY:	Oh be brave, Tammy.
TAMMY:	Did that - uh - thing, I mean did Paul . . .
SAMMY:	No, that snake didn't kill Paul.
TAMMY:	Snake! Oh dear me, dear me. I think I might faint again.
GERTRUDE:	Tammy, if you keep fainting we never will get through hearing this story. Please go on, Sammy. This is exciting.
SAMMY:	Well, Paul shook the snake off into the fire and the people that live on the island watched him. They thought that Paul was going to die.

TAMMY:	But he didn't, did he?
SAMMY:	No, he sure didn't. God was looking after him.
GERTRUDE:	How long did Paul stay on the Island of Malta? Was it for a long time?
SAMMY:	No, Paul didn't stay on the island too long. He was on the island about three months.
TAMMY:	What did Paul do all of that time?
SAMMY:	Well, the Bible tells us that Paul helped the people who lived on the island.
TAMMY:	You mean Paul helped the people on the island and he was a prisoner going to Rome?
SAMMY:	Yes, that's right, Tammy. Paul was doing what the Lord Jesus wanted him to do.
GERTRUDE:	Christians are supposed to help people everywhere aren't they, Sammy?
SAMMY:	Yes, Gertrude, the Bible teaches us that Christians are supposed to help people that are good to them and even people that are mean to them.
TAMMY:	Did Paul finally go to Rome?
SAMMY:	Oh yes, oh yes. After about three months on the Island of Malta the captain of the guards got another ship and took Paul and all the other prisoners on to Rome.
GERTRUDE:	Sammy, I believe that this is the most exciting Bible story that I have ever heard. Or at least one of the most exciting.
TAMMY:	If you ask me, it was too exciting but I still liked it.
SAMMY:	I sure am glad that you girls liked my Bible stories because Bible stories are the best stories in all the world.
TAMMY:	Boys and girls, I hope that you have learned that even when there's a storm at sea and a great shipwreck that you can trust the Lord Jesus and believe what He says.
GERTRUDE:	Boy! I'll say. Everything we read in the bible, God's Holy Word, is true and we can believe it.
SAMMY:	Right you are, girls. Well, I guess we'd better be going. When-

121

ever you girls want to hear another exciting Bible story just let me know.

TAMMY: We sure will, Sammy.

GERTRUDE: Boy! I'll say. [*All Puppets exit.*]

THE NEW JERUSALEM

Scripture:	**Revelation 21:1-27**
Characters:	**3 Puppets, 1 boy and 2 girls**

TAMMY: [*Tammy and Betty come onstage talking.*] That was a great Bible story that our teacher taught us in Sunday School last Sunday, wasn't it, Betty?

BETTY: It sure was, Tammy. Just think about it! Someday all Christians will live in the New Jerusalem.

TAMMY: Yes, it must be the most beautiful place and it will be an exciting place, too.

BETTY: I just wish that everyone knew about a beautiful place such as the New Jerusalem.

TAMMY: Oh dear me, dear me yes. I think that everyone should know about the New Jerusalem.

BETTY: The Bible says that Jesus is preparing the New Jerusalem even now so that the Christians can live there forever and ever and ever.

TAMMY: Wow! Wow! Wow! Forever and ever and ever is a long time. I mean a long, long time.

BETTY: You can say that again, Tammy.

TAMMY: Listen, Betty, what's that?

HAPPY HERMAN: [*Talking offstage.*] How happy I am! How happy I am! How happy I am! It's great to be alive today. Hooray.

BETTY: I do declare, yes, I do declare. I believe that that is Grumpy, oops, I mean Happy Herman.

TAMMY: I do believe, yes, I do believe that you are right.

BETTY: Hey, Happy Herman, come on up.

HAPPY HERMAN: [*Comes onstage talking.*] Well, well, well. It's my two best friends. How happy, how happy, how happy I am to see you. In fact, I'm just happy all the time.

BETTY: We can sure tell that, Happy Herman. You're the happiest puppet I know.

123

TAMMY:	I do indeed think you're right, Betty.
HAPPY HERMAN:	Well, it's a lot more fun being happy than being grumpy. I never, ever want to be grumpy again.
BETTY:	Well, we don't want you to be grumpy again, Happy Herman.
HAPPY HERMAN:	What are you girls doing today?
TAMMY:	Well, Happy Herman, we were just talking right before you came about the wonderful city, the New Jerusalem.
BETTY:	That's right, Happy Herman. We were talking about the wonderful city, the New Jerusalem.
HAPPY HERMAN:	The New Jerusalem. I don't think I've ever heard of that city. Is it very far away?
BETTY:	Oh dear me. The New Jerusalem is a city that Jesus is building for all Christians.
TAMMY:	That's right, Happy Herman. A most beautiful, beautiful city and Christians will live in that city forever and ever and ever.
HAPPY HERMAN:	Wow! A beautiful city where Christians will live forever and ever! Forever and ever is a long, long, long time.
BETTY:	Would you like for Tammy and me to tell you about the New Jerusalem?
HAPPY HERMAN:	Wow! Wow! My oh me, me oh my. Indeed, indeed, indeed I would. Oh yes, please tell me about the New Jerusalem.
BETTY:	All right, we'll do just that.
TAMMY:	Yes, in the Book of the Revelation we are told about the New Jerusalem. Betty, would you like to start the story of the New Jerusalem?
BETTY:	I would be delighted to, Tammy.
HAPPY HERMAN:	I would be glad for you to, too, Betty. Please go ahead and tell me about this New Jerusalem.
BETTY:	The Bible says that at the end of the world God will send down a beautiful new city called the New Jerusalem. This is going to be a city like no other city in all the world.

TAMMY:	That's right. The Bible says that in the New Jerusalem no one will ever get sick again. And there will never, never be any more pain.
HAPPY HERMAN:	Wow! Wow! Wow! Wow! What a city! You mean the Bible says all of that about the New Jerusalem?
TAMMY:	That is exactly right. The Bible says all of that. But it even says more than that.
HAPPY HERMAN:	You mean there's more?
BETTY:	There sure is. The Bible says that everything in the New Jerusalem will be perfect.
HAPPY HERMAN:	Oh dear me, oh my, oh me. You mean that no one will ever again tell a lie or do anything mean or ever be grumpy. Is that what you mean?
BETTY:	Yes, that is exactly what I mean.
HAPPY HERMAN:	Oh please tell me more.
TAMMY:	Well, the Bible also tells us that the New Jerusalem will have a wall all the way around it, and there will be twelve gates and angels will be at the gates.
BETTY:	Yes, that is true, Tammy. There will be four walls. In fact the city will be square and each wall will be 1,500 miles long.
HAPPY HERMAN:	Boy, oh boy, oh boy! That's longer than a football field. In fact, that's longer than a hundred football fields. What were these walls made out of, rocks and bricks?
BETTY:	Oh dear me, no. These walls were made out of precious stones.
TAMMY:	Betty means precious stones like jasper and sapphires and emeralds.
HAPPY HERMAN:	Oh my. I have never heard of such a city.
BETTY:	That's right, Happy Herman. There has never been a city in all the world like the New Jerusalem's going to be.
TAMMY:	That's right, never such a city. Even the gates will be made out of pearls.
HAPPY HERMAN:	You mean all twelve gates will be made out of pearls?

TAMMY:	That's right, Happy Herman. All twelve gates will be made out of pearls. Those will be the most beautiful gates that anyone has ever seen.
BETTY:	But that's not all.
HAPPY HERMAN:	I can hardly believe it. You mean there's even more?
TAMMY:	Oh dear me yes. The Bible also says that the streets of the New Jerusalem will be paved with gold.
HAPPY HERMAN:	You mean real gold? That yellow stuff?
TAMMY:	That's right.
HAPPY HERMAN:	Well, this is going to be the best city that there ever was.
BETTY:	But I haven't told you the most important thing about the New Jerusalem yet, Happy Herman.
TAMMY:	Yes, the best part is yet to come.
HAPPY HERMAN:	The best part is yet to come? The best part is yet to come? What more, what more, what more could there be?
BETTY:	The Bible tells us that there'll be no church because the Lord will be the center of the city and there'll be no need for a church.
TAMMY:	Yes, yes, yes, that's right. And in the New Jerusalem there will be no sun or moon because the Lord will be the light.
HAPPY HERMAN:	Oh my, oh my, oh my. How wonderful, how wonderful, how wonderful. I've got two questions about this city.
BETTY:	What are they?
TAMMY:	Yes, what are they? We'll try to answer them if we can.
HAPPY HERMAN:	My first question is: if there's not going to be any sun or moon and the Lord's going to be the light, will there be a daytime and a nighttime?
BETTY:	That's a good question, Happy Herman. The Bible does give us the answer to your question.
HAPPY HERMAN:	What is the answer? Do tell me, what is the answer?
BETTY:	The Bible says that there will never again be any night because the Lord will be the light forever and ever and ever in

the New Jerusalem.

HAPPY HERMAN: Wow! Wow! Wow! No more night! That'll be great, great, great.

TAMMY: What's your next question, Happy Herman?

HAPPY HERMAN: Tammy, my next question is: how will the Lord know who belongs in the New Jerusalem?

TAMMY: The Bible says that all who have their names written in the Lamb's Book of Life will live in the New Jerusalem.

BETTY: That means that everyone who is really a Christian and has let Jesus become his Saviour has his name written in the Lamb's Book of Life in Heaven.

HAPPY HERMAN: Oh, how wonderful, how wonderful, how wonderful! I wish everybody had their names written in the Lamb's Book of Life so they could live in the New Jerusalem.

BETTY: Yes, I do too.

TAMMY: Me too, me too.

HAPPY HERMAN: Thank you, girls, for telling me such an exciting story about the New Jerusalem. I must hurry along now because I want to tell all my friends about the New Jerusalem. I'll see you again real soon. [*Herman exits.*]

TAMMY: Wow! Wow! Wow! Happy Herman was really happy, wasn't he?

BETTY: Yes, he was. And boys and girls if you have your name written in the Lamb's Book of Life you can be happy, too, because someday you can live in the New Jerusalem.

TAMMY: How true, how true, Betty. Let's go and see if we can't find someone else to tell about the New Jerusalem.

BETTY: That would really be neat. Let's do. [*Both Puppets exit.*]